Epworth

Gen
Ivor H. Jones

The Epistle to the Philippians

The Epistle to the
PHILIPPIANS

HOWARD MARSHALL

EPWORTH PRESS

ISBN 0 7162 0485 1

First Published 1992
by Epworth Press
1 Central Buildings Westminster
London SW1H 9NR

Typeset by Regent Typesetting, London
and printed in Finland by
Werner Söderström Oy

CONTENTS

Contents

GENERAL INTRODUCTION

The *Epworth Preacher's Commentaries* that Greville P. Lewis edited so successfully in the 1950s and 1960s having now served their turn, the Epworth Press has commissioned a team of distinguished academics who are also preachers and teachers to create a new series of commentaries that will serve the 1990s and beyond. We have seized the opportunity offered by the publication in 1989 of the Revised English Bible to use this very readable and scholarly version as the basis of our commentaries, and we are grateful to the Oxford and Cambridge University Presses for the requisite licence and for granting our authors pre-publication access. They will nevertheless be free to cite and discuss other translations wherever they think that these will illuminate the original text.

Just as the books that make up the Bible differ in their provenance and purpose, so our authors will necessarily differ in the structure and bearing of their commentaries. But they will all strive to get as close as possible to the intention of the original writers, expounding their texts in the light of the place, time, circumstances, and culture that gave them birth, and showing why each work was received by Jews and Christians into their respective Canons of Holy Scripture. They will seek to make full use of the dramatic advance in biblical scholarship world-wide but at the same time to explain technical terms in the language of the common reader, and to suggest ways in which Scripture can help towards the living of a Christian life today. They will endeavour to produce commentaries that can be used with confidence in ecumenical, multiracial, and multifaith situations, and not by scholars only but by preachers, teachers, students, church members, and anyone who wants to improve his or her understanding of the Bible.

Ivor H. Jones

PREFACE

This commentary is especially intended to encourage preachers to preach from the letter of Paul to the Philippians and to help them in their task. Our concern is with biblical preaching, and more specifically with the kind of preaching which is based on a particular word, text or passage in a biblical book. (There are other kinds of preaching which use the Bible in different ways, but we do not need to consider these here.)

The actual preparation of a sermon can begin in a variety of ways. Basically, there are two approaches. The one begins with a biblical text, and asks the question: What has this text to say to us in our situation today? The other begins with us in some particular situation (which may perhaps be unknown to the biblical writers) and asks: Has the Bible any light to shed on our situation? But whether the starting point is the biblical text or some modern situation, the basic underlying question is how one moves from the ancient text to the contemporary sermon. In other words, if personal choice or some programme such as a lectionary requires the preacher to say something about the message of Philippians, what are the essential tasks involved in preparing a sermon? Let me suggest three:

(1) *Exegesis.* The basic question is concerned with what we might call the 'message' of the text for a modern congregation. How does one find a message in what was originally written for first-century readers for a somewhat different audience? It is not an adequate answer to that question to say that what the biblical writers wrote is the Word of God and therefore it is a timeless message for people of all times; that answer still leaves us asking how we find out what the Word of God in a particular passage is. Fortunately, it seems to be agreed by all serious students that we can understand what the text *is saying* to us today only in the light of an understanding of what the text *was saying* to its original readers. What was Paul saying to the Philippian church?

To answer that question is the task of *biblical exegesis*, and this is in fact what you will find in the average commentary. It will try to put us into the situation of Paul's readers so that we can read the letter with their eyes; it will explain any difficulties that arise because we are modern people and do not know what was in the minds of the Philippians that enabled them to understand what Paul was saying; and it will attempt to clarify any things in the text that might also have been obscure to the original readers. In doing so it will use all the techniques of study which can throw light on the text.

(2) *Exposition*. The problem for the preacher with many commentaries, however, is that many commentators have not seen it as their duty to go any further than this; the restrictions imposed by the space available or by the aims of a commentary series, coupled with the feeling that it is somehow 'unscientific' to study the Bible as if it were any different from any other book, ancient or modern, have meant that the majority of commentaries are exegetical and nothing more. Now fortunately there is a reversal of the trend, and some series of commentaries are beginning to recognize that the commentator's duty is not done until the message of the text for today has been teased out.

In other words, the commentator must ask the question: What has what Paul said to the Philippians got to say to the congregation in Little Street Methodist Church next Sunday morning at 11.0 am when I am preaching to them? The question is unavoidable because our congregations are not the Philippians and the teaching of the letter needs what we call 'interpretation' if it is to function as God's Word today. It will not do to say that, if the commentator has done his work properly, the readers themselves will perceive the questions of faith and morals which arise. They may well not perceive the questions, and even less may they on occasion be able to work out the answers. I am increasingly of the opinion that the commentator must say something on these matters. The preacher needs some guidance on interpreting the text for today.

There is, to be sure, a kind of preaching which simply re-tells the Bible stories or describes to the congregation what Paul was telling the Philippians to do. But, valuable though this may be as entertainment or historical teaching, it is not really preaching and it ought not to be honoured by the name. Preaching is presenting the Word of God for the congregation to the congregation. But it cannot be done without some help and guidance.

To a considerable extent, of course, the commentator is limited in the help that can be offered. For he may know the text but he doesn't know the particular congregation that I have to face next Sunday morning. It has been said that to teach Johnny arithmetic the teacher must know arithmetic – and Johnny. As commentator, I do not know the specific congregation whom you are trying to instruct. All, therefore, that can be done is to offer some rather general comments based on my knowledge of the world in which I live and of the congregations to which I preach, in the confidence that yours will be sufficiently similar to make my comments helpful to you.

(3) *Presentation.* There is a third question which arises once we have interpreted the text for today, and that is the question of how to put it across most effectively to the actual congregation: the question, in short, of how to prepare and preach the sermon in such a way that it is interesting, instructive and persuasive. This task is not attempted in this commentary. I have not included any sermons, although from time to time I have tried to structure and number the points discussed so that they might form the basis for sermon 'outlines'.

Recently I saw a programme for a set of talks on the letter with the general title 'Realistic Godliness in Philippians' and the individual titles: Coping in an Unfair World; Shining in a Crooked World; Growing in a Christless World; Contented in a Materialistic World. This is a good example of how to present the message of the four chapters of this letter, but it represents the stage of attractive and memorable presentation which I am perforce leaving to the reader.

So the task of actually making sermons is not being discussed here; I offer no more than the raw material which can be used. You can read books of sermons based on the letter – such as the outstanding work of D. M. Lloyd-Jones – and you will see how the 'expert' goes about it. It may be daunting to read such a work, especially since a Lloyd-Jones sermon was about twice the length of an average Methodist sermon. (But it might be no bad thing to wean our congregations away from the belief that once twenty minutes have passed the preacher is into 'extra time'!). Nevertheless, the preacher can learn a lot from studying the technique of a master.

We are, then, to concentrate on the first two stages of the process in this commentary, to provide the essential spadework that the preacher should go through before attempting to construct an actual sermon. Some of the material presented will be slightly more technical, concerned with establishing just what Paul was trying to say, and discussing different alternatives put forward by commentators.

This is part of the preacher's 'homework' and is not generally appropriate for a congregation, and I have put it in smaller type. Some of the exegesis will form the basis of straightforward material for preaching, because the line between what Paul was saying to the Philippians and what he is saying to us is often a thin one. And some of the material will be more obviously interpretation where I have tried to do such things as summing up more systematically particular themes that arise in the letter, indicating points that can well be applied to congregations today, and above all discussing places where the material raises problems and needs to be given a fresh exposition and application if it is to be usable today. Material that is more obviously concerned with 'exposition' and 'application' is generally indented in the text, but often exegesis and interpretation can hardly be separated.

I have not included references to the scholars who have helped me by their writings, but every page is indebted to the work of others. I am particularly grateful to my wife, Joyce, for help with the proofs, and to Miss Jean Cunningham, formerly of the SCM Press, who prepared the book for publication.

I have so filled up the space available to me that no room has been left for a dedicatory page. Therefore, I conclude this Preface by saying that this book is for Patrick and Ruth Edwards in gratitude for their fellowship and friendship over many years.

BIBLIOGRAPHY

This bibliography is divided into three parts. First, out of the abundance of helpful commentaries on Philippians, I have listed those which are most easily accessible and helpful for the preacher (and which make little or no reference to Greek words). Second, a list of more technical commentaries which have been used in preparation of this commentary is included. Third, I have listed those essays which I have found most useful.

1. Helps for the preacher

Commentaries on the letter

F. W. Beare, *Philippians* (Black's NT Commentaries), London: A. & C. Black, 2nd edition 1969; now showing the signs of its age.

F. F. Bruce, *Philippians* (Good News Bible Commentary), Basingstoke: Pickering and Inglis 1984; republished in New International Bible Commentary, Peabody, Mass.: Hendrickson 1989; excellent short commentary.

G. B. Caird, *Paul's Letters from Prison* (New Clarendon Bible), Oxford University Press, 1976; brief but helpful comments.

J. L. Houlden, *Paul's Letters from Prison*, Harmondsworth: Penguin Books, 1967; a good alternative to Caird.

R. P. Martin, *Philippians* (Tyndale NT Commentaries), Leicester: Inter-Varsity Press revised edition, 1987; good up-to-date work by a specialist.

— *Philippians* (New Century Bible), London: Marshall Pickering, revised edition, 1983; somewhat fuller than his other commentary.

Expositions of the letter

D. M. Lloyd-Jones, *The Life of Joy* and *The Life of Peace*, London: Hodder & Stoughton 1989 and 1990; expository sermons by an outstanding preacher.

J. A. Motyer, *The Message of Philippians: Jesus our Joy*, Leicester: Inter-Varsity Press 1984; a soundly based application of the letter to modern readers.

Books on the theology of Philippians

G. F. Hawthorne, *Word Biblical Themes: Philippians*, Waco: Word Books 1987; excellent summary of teaching on the main themes in the letter.

K. P. Donfried and I. H. Marshall, *The Shorter Paulines: Thessalonians, Philippians and Philemon* (New Testament Theology Vol. 10), Cambridge University Press, forthcoming; a systematic exposition of Paul's theology as expressed in the letter.

2. *Commentaries requiring knowledge of Greek:*

J.-F. Collange, *The Epistle of Saint Paul to the Philippians*, Eng. trs, London: Epworth Press 1979; learned work by a distinguished French scholar; rather technical.

G. F. Hawthorne, *Philippians* (Word Biblical Commentary), Waco: Word Books 1983; very full and readable exegesis with constant reference to the Greek text.

P. O'Brien, *Philippians* (New International Greek Testament Commentary), Grand Rapids: Eerdmans 1991; extremely detailed, sound exegesis based on the Greek text throughout.

M. Silva, *Philippians* (Wycliffe Exegetical Commentary), Chicago: Moody Press, 1988; essentially a discussion of the Greek text.

3. Essays and other works on technical points

D. E. Garland, 'The Composition and Unity of Philippians. Some Neglected Literary Factors', *Novum Testamentum* 27, 1985, 141–173.

R. P. Martin, *Carmen Christi: Philippians 2:5–11 in recent interpretation and in the setting of early Christian worship*, Grand Rapids: Eerdmans, 2nd edition, 1983; highly technical study of a single passage.

Duane F. Watson, 'A Rhetorical Analysis of Philippians and its Implications for the Unity Question', *Novum Testamentum* 30, 1988, 57–88.

N. T. Wright, '*Harpagmos* and the meaning of Philippians 2:5–11', *Journal of Theological Studies* n.s. 37, 1986, 321–352; very important scholarly discussion.

ABBREVIATIONS

GNB   Good News Bible, 1976
JB   Jerusalem Bible, 1966
NEB   New English Bible, 1970
NIV   New International Version of the Bible, 1979
NRSV   New Revised Standard Version of the Bible, 1990
NT   New Testament
OT   Old Testament
REB   Revised English Bible, 1989

INTRODUCTION

Philippi and Paul's Mission

Philippi was an ancient town in the country in the north of modern Greece which was called Macedonia in ancient times. The town was given its name by Philip of Macedon, the father of Alexander the Great (c. 360 BC). In 42 BC it was the site of a famous battle in which Antony and Octavian (later to become the Roman Emperor Augustus) defeated the troops of Brutus and Cassius (the murderers of Julius Caesar). The victors made the town into a Roman colony, i.e. a place where veteran soldiers could settle on demobilization and enjoy the privileges of self-government and freedom from taxation. This move injected new life into the town, and had the effect of turning a Greek town into one with a more strongly Roman character. After the defeat of Antony and Cleopatra in 31 BC further veterans were settled there. Luke aptly describes it in Acts 16.12 as 'a leading city in that district of Macedonia and a Roman colony'. There do not appear to have been many Jews in the town.

After Paul had had his vision summoning him to Macedonia (Acts 16.9f.), he and Silas came here from Asia. They met up with a number of Jewish women, including a business woman named Lydia, and their message met with an encouraging reception. Lydia was baptized and opened her house to them. Paul continued to visit the Jewish 'place of prayer', and the story tells how he came into contact with a slave girl who had the gift of telling fortunes and exorcized her of the evil spirit which was believed to inhabit her. The incident annoyed the girl's owners, who doubtless made a good profit out of her. A riot ensued, and the missionaries were arrested and brought before the local magistrates on a complaint of 'un-Roman' conduct. They were given a beating (an illegal procedure in the case of Roman citizens) and thrown into prison. During the night there was an earthquake; the jailer feared that his prisoners had escaped and was prepared to kill himself rather than face the consequences, but was stopped by Paul who spoke to him and brought him to faith. The following morning the missionaries were set free, but they did not go without demanding an apology for their unlawful treatment. Nevertheless, they lost no time in leaving the town and moving on to the next major centre, Thessalonica.

Such is the story related by Luke (Acts 16.11–40). Some parts of it have been thought to contain legendary elements, but there is no good reason to question the essential core of it. The person who wrote the parts of Acts related in the first person was evidently present for some part of the time (Acts 16.12–17; cf. 20.6)

When he left Philippi, Paul travelled south through Achaia (the southern part of modern Greece) to Athens and Corinth, where he spent at least eighteen months. He then crossed over to Ephesus, paid a flying visit to Caesarea and Antioch, and returned to Ephesus where he spent more than two years in evangelism. Then he journeyed north to Macedonia, and (although it is not explicitly mentioned) he must doubtless have visited Philippi (Acts 20.1f.). He then went on south to Greece and stayed in Corinth.

Paul's plans to return from Corinth direct to Jerusalem were changed at the last minute, and he decided to return to Macedonia. In Acts 20.6 we read how he sailed from Philippi to Troas on the first stage of his journey to Jerusalem for what turned out to be his final visit.

In between the initial visit and these two visits we know that Paul's colleagues Timothy and Erastus visited Macedonia (Acts 19.22). It is also probable that Timothy or Silas visited Philippi earlier, immediately after Paul first left the town (cf. Acts 17.14). When Paul referred to 'the churches in Macedonia' and their generosity despite their difficult situation in II Cor. 8 – 9, he was doubtless thinking of the church in Philippi.

This is as much as we know about the history of Paul's dealings with the church apart from and before the writing of the letter. Unfortunately, it does not shed much light on the letter itself as regards the specific events that gave rise to it.

The place and date of writing

Where was Paul when he wrote the letter? He was in prison (Phil. 1.13, 17) and he recognized the possibility of his imminent death, although he believed that he would continue to live and serve the

Lord (1.20–26). If the death he feared was death by execution, then he must have been imprisoned in Rome; a Roman citizen (which, according to Acts 22.25–28, Paul was) with the right of appeal to Caesar, could not be legally executed away from Rome.

Other evidence in the letter fits this assumption. The 'imperial guard' (Gk. *praitōrion* = Latin *praetorium*) in 1.13 will be the members of the praetorian regiment who were stationed in Rome, and in 4.22 'those in the emperor's service' (lit. 'Caesar's household') will be members of the imperial civil service.

In this case the letter will belong to the period at the end of Paul's life when he was imprisoned in Rome (Acts 28) and will have been written several years after the foundation of the church.

But this reconstruction is open to some doubt. It has been noted that several messages and messengers passed between Philippi and Paul, and it has been argued that the difficulties in communication and the length of the journey make Rome seem unlikely. The reference to the gifts Paul received from Philippi when he first worked in Macedonia and the suggestion that only now 'after so long' – several years later – the church had helped him again (4.10, 15) seems inappropriate, if not impolite. Could the letter be redated?

The only other imprisonment of Paul for any length of time recorded in Acts is in Caesarea, and this could possibly be the place from which he wrote. The word *praetorium* can then have its other meaning of a governor's HQ (such as existed in Caesarea), and 'Caesar's household' refers to travelling diplomats. The letter is brought nearer in time to the mission to Philippi. But the difficulty, if any, in the long journeys still remains, and, more importantly, we do not know that Paul expected to be set free in Caesarea and able to visit Philippi again. A compelling case for preferring Caesarea to Rome has not yet been offered.

However, since we know that Paul was frequently imprisoned (II Cor. 11.23), it can be assumed that he was imprisoned in other places, and Ephesus emerges as a likely place in view of the length of time Paul spent there and the vigorous opposition which he experienced. It is indeed perfectly possible that he was imprisoned there. The case for Ephesus as then being the place from which Philippians was written has been strongly and widely defended, not least because of the proximity of the two towns. If the letter was written from here, it would of course be much nearer in time to the founding of the church.

There is, however, an objection which F. F. Bruce regards as fatal.

This is that 'there is no known instance in imperial times of its use [sc. the use of *'praetorium'*] for the headquarters of a proconsul, the governor of a senatorial province such as Asia was at this time.'[1] If this linguistic point is correct, the Ephesian hypothesis must drop out of discussion, whatever its other merits and attractions. That is how I propose to treat it, without discussing in detail the other arguments for and against the hypothesis.

The situation giving rise to the letter

We must now tackle the question of the circumstances which led to the composition of the letter. There are two sides to this, Paul's own position and the situation of the church. Paul wrote because of what had been happening to himself, especially as it affected the church at Philippi, and also because of what he had heard about the needs of the church.

Paul's own situation

Paul had been in prison, evidently for some period of time. The members of the church at Philippi had an especially close relationship to him and regarded themselves as his partners in the work of the gospel. They had entered into an arrangement to provide him with financial help in the early days of the church, and had sent money to him in Thessalonica. When they heard of his imprisonment, they sent another monetary gift to him by the hand of Epaphroditus, who was one of their own Christian group. Epaphroditus fell ill, whether on his way to Paul or after he arrived. The illness was sufficiently severe and lengthy for there to be great concern over him at Philippi. (This implies that news about him travelled back to Philippi.) Epaphroditus was anxious over the effect that the news of his illness would have on the church. (It is not clear whether Paul is here referring to his very natural assumption that this would be the case or to the arrival of a further message from Philippi expressing the anxiety of the church. The former is perhaps more probable, since no mention is made in the letter of the arrival of any other messengers.) Paul, therefore, decided that it was best for Epaphroditus to return home instead of staying on to assist him, and the letter was written to accompany him back home.

From the letter we also learn that Timothy was soon to visit Philippi, and it was Paul's hope that he would be able to return with news of the church. All this, however, was only a preliminary to a possible visit by Paul himself. He intended to delay sending Timothy until he had a better idea of his own future, and he was confident that that future would include the possibility of his own return to Philippi.

We can thus explain the direct occasion of the letter quite simply in terms of these circumstances. But we have still to explain the particular things that Paul says in the letter. On the one hand, he naturally wanted to give news about himself and his own situation to his friends. It may be that rumours were circulating about his imprisonment and its effects. His friends would naturally assume that his detention would hinder his work as a Christian missionary. Paul wanted to assure them that this was not the case, that the reasons for his imprisonment had become known to the people round about and had thus provided an opportunity for witness, and that other Christians in the area had taken fresh courage from Paul's example to proclaim Christ. (He admitted that some were doing so from the wrong motives, but that didn't worry him unduly.)

At the same time, there was naturally concern about how his imprisonment would end. It must be remembered that imprisonment in the ancient world was used as a means of keeping people in custody until their trial and not as a form of sentence (except for situations like debt). Paul evidently anticipated the possibility of execution, and had come to terms with it. But he knew that his friends were praying for him, and he expressed his confidence that the answer to their prayers would be his deliverance and consequently the opportunity for him to give them further help. All this had to be explained to the readers.

The situation and needs of the church

At the same time, there were things to be said about their situation, advice and help to be given to them immediately without waiting for his future visit to them. Alongside his general concern for their spiritual welfare Paul was worried about some particular problems.

(a) *Tensions within the church* First, there was quarrelling in the church – two ladies are specifically named in this connection (4.2), but it had spread more widely. It is quite likely that the two named persons occupied leading roles in the church, and that some of the members had lined up in support of them. If church groups met in their respective homes, this would have helped to foment divisions and rivalries. This letter is very much the letter of Christian unity, in which the church is urged to live at peace within itself.

We do not know for certain what was causing the tensions. It is clear that there was a problem. It may have been due simply to ordinary human causes – to the petty jealousies and rivalries which can develop in any close-knit society. It is possible that, if the church was being made the object of attack from outside, then there was tension over how to respond, with some people taking a hard line and others an easier line. Three particular suggestions should be mentioned. One is that there was some dissension over the role of Epaphroditus, between those who approved of his mission to Paul and those who disagreed and pointed to its apparent lack of success. (Why does Paul go to such pains to commend him to the church?) A second possibility is that the figure of Paul himself was causing debate, with some people claiming that the fact that he was in prison was a sign that he was unsuccessful as an apostle while others were upholding his reputation. Yet another possibility is that the pressure on the church from outside and possibly the claim of some of the church members to be a kind of spiritual elite were causing tension (see below). There may be elements of truth in all these suggestions, but we probably should admit that we do not know for certain the underlying causes. Ordinary human bickering may be a sufficient explanation; it certainly is in many churches today!

(b) *Attacks on the church*. Second, the church was experiencing pressure of some kind, so that Paul can speak of it being called to 'suffer' for Christ. The reference is probably to the general hostility which Christians might face at any time in the ancient world, but it may also include the people mentioned in 3.18 as 'enemies of the cross of Christ'. Organized persecution of the church by the government was not a factor at this time, but Christians might well find themselves being discriminated against and suffering verbal abuse and other harassment from their neighbours. We may well suspect that Paul's frequent appeals in the letter to them to be joyful reflect a situation in which they were feeling unduly depressed.

(c) *A rival version of the gospel.* Third, there was a group of people who constituted a danger to church, and against whom Paul writes with some vehemence. This happens in ch. 3. First, in 3.2 Paul warns his readers to beware of a group whom he describes variously as 'those dogs, those who do nothing but harm and who insist on mutilation'. He draws a contrast between them and Christians who are 'the circumcision', i.e. 'the true circumcision'. He suggests that the people whom he is opposing put their confidence in the physical, namely in the marks of Jewish piety and zeal. Later on he puts himself forward as an example to follow, and he warns against people who are enemies of the cross, 'who make appetite their god' and 'take pride in what should bring shame' (3.19).

Who were these people? An immediate problem is whether Paul is thinking of one group of people or of two. But it will be best to look at what is said about each group before deciding on a solution to this problem. Three things are said about them at the beginning of the chapter.

1. 'Dogs' was an insulting term used by Jews for Gentiles. It is generally thought that Paul is throwing it back at Jews who were attacking the gospel with its insistence that Gentiles did not need to be circumcised or keep the Jewish law.

2. 'Those who do nothing but harm' is literally 'evil workers' and refers to missionaries. This suggests that they are rivals and opponents of Paul whom he attacks more strongly than the rivals in ch. 1. It also makes it probable that these were people who were not native members of the church at Philippi but were part of a group of travelling missionaries who followed in Paul's footsteps. But it is not clear whether the group had actually visited Philippi. There is no indication that any of the members of the church had succumbed to their teaching. They appear to be a potential danger, but nevertheless one that needed to be strongly guarded against.

3. Those 'who insist on mutilation' must be a bitter pun on 'circumcisers'. These were people who practised circumcision, or else Paul would not contrast it with the Christian circumcision in the next verse. In all probability they urged circumcision upon Gentile Christians.

This description is virtually certain to be that of so-called Judaizing Christians, people who claimed to be Christians in that they accepted Jesus as the Messiah but who held strongly that to be 'proper' Christians and members of the people of God *all* Christians had to be circumcised and observe the Jewish law. It appears that people with this outlook dogged Paul's footsteps and tried to persuade his converts that what Paul had told them was insufficient. They put their trust in the physical – in the outward signs of religiosity, including circumcision – and they went about urging this message on the Gentile Christians. They were similar in outlook to the opponents whom Paul attacks in Galatians, whom he accused of preaching a different gospel and of making the cross useless.

> Another possibility is that these people were non-Christian Jews who were trying to persuade Paul's Gentile converts to accept Judaism rather than Christianity, but the description fits Jewish Christian missionaries better.

Now let us consider what is said about the people in vv. 17ff. They have been variously identified as:

(a) Pagan non-believers who were opposed to the Christian church and all that it stood for.

(b) Judaizing Christians who are the same people as those attacked at the beginning of the chapter.

(c) People who held that Christians were not bound by any moral laws and could live as they pleased.

Since Paul is singling out a particular group, it is unlikely that he is referring to unbelievers in general, and therefore view (a) can probably be dismissed. It would also be strange if Paul were to introduce a fresh group of opponents at this point without any clear signals that he was doing so.

This suggests that view (b) is more probable. In view of the similarity between them and the opponents of Paul in Galatians, the description of them as 'enemies of the cross' will fit. And when we compare the strong language that Paul used against such people in Galatians 1.8f. it is quite conceivable that Paul could say that they were 'heading for destruction'.

The difficult phrase on this view is 'making appetite their god'. However, the Greek word *koilia* can refer to several physical organs and not simply to the stomach. It can be used euphemistically for the sexual organ, so that Paul may be saying that they regard their circumcision as an idol. 'Taking pride in what should bring them shame' can be equated with vaunting their circumcision. And 'setting their minds on earthly things' can refer to boasting in the human, outward signs of Judaism.

It could also be argued that this description rather favours view (c), namely that Paul is referring to people who were living immoral lives, indulging in bodily pleasures and sins, and perhaps vaunting their freedom to do so. We know of Christians at Corinth who thought that various bodily sins were quite compatible with a Christian profession (I Cor. 5.11; 6.9f.) We should also note that Paul uses similar language in Rom. 16.17f. about people who 'serve their own appetites' and cause divisions in the church by attempting to persuade other people to live in the same kind of way. Unfortunately it is very hard to identify just whom Paul has in mind in this passage. It may also be significant that in Galatians we have clear warnings against falling into bodily sins (Gal. 5.13–21). It may be, therefore, that a stress on Judaizing coupled with less emphasis on the cross could be associated with a lax attitude towards sin.

From all this it emerges that we can probably identify the people described in the earlier part of the chapter (3.1–11) as Judaizers. However, the view that the same group of people are also in view in 3.17ff. is not so certain. It is also arguable that here we have a group of people who believed that they could indulge their physical desires to the limit and in this way were failing to live according to the way of the cross.

We should also note that in the middle of the chapter (3.12–16) Paul refers to a group who thought of themselves as 'mature', and it may be that this refers to people who thought that one had to go on beyond the message of the cross to acceptance of Judaism in order to be a full, 'mature' Christian. They may have thought that maturity and sin were not incompatible.

It may seem curious that, if Paul felt so strongly about these people, he left off mentioning them until fairly late on in the letter and in effect interrupted what he was saying about unity in the church. The situation is not unlike that in II Cor. 10 – 13, where Paul also deals with a trouble not hinted at in the earlier part of the letter. This may suggest that Paul was dealing with a threat to the church rather than a reality in its midst. He is warning the church against outsiders who may attack it, preparing them in advance for an attack, and therefore this matter was not so urgent as the problems affecting himself and the church.

In any case, Paul's aim in this part of the letter is certainly warning, but he uses it to present a positive contrast in the shape of authentic Christian living which is patterned on Christ and which finds standing with God in the righteousness that comes from the work of Christ on the cross.

It is probable that what Paul says in this chapter has some links with the rest of the letter. It is true that we do not need the threat of this false teaching as an explanation for the disunity in the church. The disunity appears to arise primarily out of selfishness and unloving attitudes rather than out of doctrinal disagreements. However, the attitude in ch. 2 is partly at least one of looking down on other believers, a lack of humility; this would tie in with the fact that some people considered themselves 'mature' in 3.14 and may have looked down on others. Probably 3.12–16 is concerned with people in the church and is not connected directly with the opponents. But it may be evidence of an attitude or disposition to which the false teaching might appeal.

In particular, it may well be that the teaching about Jesus in 2.5–11 is relevant to what is developed later in ch. 3. It could be that part of the reason for emphasizing the exaltation of Jesus Christ as Lord was to prepare the way for emphasizing how Christians must be conformed to the pattern of his suffering, and must set their hopes on resurrection to be with him when he comes as 'the Lord Jesus Christ' and be concerned to experience the transformation of their fleshly bodies into glorious bodies at that time.

The contents and structure of the letter

Our next task is to try to understand what is going on in the letter as a whole. Can we trace the flow of thought in the letter? Does it have a developing argument? Does it have several themes in different sections? Or is it unplanned, as at least one commentator suggests, like a conversation that moves from one topic to another more by association of ideas and words than by any more exact kind of logic? So far, in trying to work out the situation of the letter, we have been engaged in what is sometimes called 'mirror-reading' – trying to gain a picture of the community addressed from the image of it that is presented in the letter. We have assumed that the letter is meant to deal with the needs arising from the situation of the author in relation to the readers and of the readers in relation to him. We therefore are working in the expectation that the content of the letter is shaped by these needs. But it may also be shaped by the requirements of a particular pattern of writing.

There is more than one possible approach to the problem before us.

Philippians as a letter

The most obvious starting point is that we are dealing with a letter. Ancient letters, like modern ones, followed a set pattern and any letter-writer would feel bound by these conventions, even if there was freedom for variation.

Ancient letters can generally be divided up into a main part called the 'body' preceded by an introductory salutation and followed by closing greetings. It was not uncommon for the body to begin with a statement of the writer's prayers or good wishes for the readers.

Philippians clearly falls into this pattern, with the Christian development of the salutation (1.1–2) and closing greetings (4.21–23) that is familiar from Paul's other letters. However, this analysis does not take us very far when we try to analyse the body more closely. We can detect the presence of various types of material which were common in ancient letters – such as the opening expression of good wishes or prayer (1.3–11), statements about the writer's own situation (1.12–26), discussion of a forthcoming visit to the recipients (2.19–30), and exhortation or instruction (e.g. 4.2–9). But recognition of the formal 'shape' of the letter does not help us greatly to understand what is going on in it, any more than recognition of, say, the broad shape of a musical composition like a symphony or sonata takes us far in understanding just what the composer has achieved within the constraints of a particular structure.

Philippians as an example of rhetoric

A different type of approach is again concerned with the formal structure of the letter. Recent scholars have examined various books of the New Testament and analysed them against what is known of the theory and practices of ancient rhetoric. This approach presupposes that the essential shape and content of Philippians is that of a written speech in which the writer behaves like an ancient orator who is attempting to persuade his audience of some proposition.

Ancient speeches were classified into three different types, namely:
   a. Judicial, concerned with accusation and defence.
   b. Deliberative, concerned with persuasion and dissuasion.
   c. Epideictic, concerned with praise and blame.

Broadly speaking, the first of these was used in a court, the second in political meetings, and the third in ceremonial gatherings. Philippians has been interpreted as 'deliberative', its aim being to show what kind of life is worthy of the gospel.

Speeches fell into a formal pattern with various elements known by Latin names. It will be simplest to explain the pattern with specific reference to Philippians. It can be structured as follows:

INTRODUCTION (*Exordium*) (*1.3–26*) This section was intended to secure the goodwill of the audience for the speaker and to prepare the way for the main subject.

THEME (*Narratio*) (*1.27–30*) This is a statement of the concerns for which the exordium has prepared the way. It contains in effect the proposition which will be elaborated and defended in the rest of the speech. The Philippians are to live a life that is worthy of the gospel and to stand firm and united against any opponents.

ARGUMENT (*Probatio*) (*2.1 – 3.21*) This is the heart of the speech, offering arguments and examples to support the case. Various argumentative devices are used. The section can be subdivided into three main parts with a 'digression':

FIRST DEVELOPMENT (*2.1–11*). After the proposition has been restated, the argument is reinforced by an example, that of Christ himself.

SECOND DEVELOPMENT (*2.12–18*). Here Paul appeals to his own authority and example.

DIGRESSION (*Digressio*) (*2.19–30*) Although logically a digression from the argument of the letter, this section aids the argument by exemplifying the kind of life that is desired in the readers. It is not recounting material about Timothy and Epaphroditus simply out of general interest but basically in order to show how the readers should live.

THIRD DEVELOPMENT (*3.1–21*) This section again contains argument by example (that of Paul himself) but also by attacking directly a different way of life which is contrary to the gospel.

FINAL APPEAL (*Peroratio*) (*4.1–20*) The speech reaches its climax in a 'peroration' which is intended to sum up the argument and press it home. It has two parts:

RECAPITULATION (*Repetitio*) (*4.1–9*) The basic points are repeated in a way that picks up what has already been said, and also expresses it in a fresh way.

APPEAL (*Adfectus*) (*4.10–20*) An emotional appeal to the readers serves to arouse an emotional attachment to the speaker and hence to encourage agreement with his case.

If this proposed outline (developed by D. F. Watson) is correct, it shows that a unified theme can be detected right through the letter from end to end. However, it is probably too neat.

Analysis by content

Rhetorical analysis is formal in nature, and basically it shows the function of the different parts of the letter,. However, it inevitably depends on the content of the various sections, and it is here that some problems arise. We may wonder whether the content of the letter is sometimes being forced into a mould which it does not altogether fit. As Watson himself admits, the 'appeal' is rather veiled in its character. I find it hard to believe that the material about Timothy and Epaphroditus is used primarily as an example for the readers. The assumption being made is that the letter really has only one theme, rather than multiple functions. But surely Paul had things to say about himself and his colleagues which were not merely means of raising sympathy and a receptive spirit for what was to follow. Doubtless he could use this material to instruct and encourage the readers, but it seems unlikely that he introduced it only for this purpose. Watson is right to recognize that 1.27–30 is the key to the main theme in Paul's teaching to the Philippians. But not everything in the letter is necessarily tied to that one theme.

A looser analysis of the letter would be as follows:

1.1 – 2	OPENING GREETING	
1.3 – 4.20	BODY OF THE LETTER	
1.3–11		Opening prayer-report
1.12–26		Paul's own situation and prospects
1.27 – 2.18		Appeal for unity and humility within the church
2.19–30		Future visits to Philippi by Paul and his colleagues
3.1 – 4.1		Warning against Judaizers
4.2 – 9		Practical instructions for life in the church
4.10–20		Thanks for a gift to Paul
4.21–23	CLOSING GREETINGS	

This analysis attempts to do justice to the letter as a letter with the prayer-report as part of the letter structure. The basic divisions in the letter are fairly clear and correspond to those of Watson. The difference is that we are not claiming that they form a tight rhetorical structure.

On this view, Paul begins the letter with a prayer-report in which he indicates that two themes are on his mind: first, the work of the gospel in which he and the readers share, and which may seem to be hindered by his imprisonment; and, second, the spiritual growth of the readers in love (1.3–11).

He then moves on to a section in which he discusses the first of these topics, explaining the problems in his own situation and showing how these are not really problems in that the gospel is being proclaimed and he himself is confident that he will continue his work rather than being snatched away from it (however desirable it might be to depart and be more closely with Christ) (1.12–26).

From this thought of his continuing care for the churches he moves to the particular instruction which he wishes to give the Philippians, which is concerned with their living a life worthy of the gospel, and specifically in living together in unity, being prepared for any suffering that might result, and withstanding any opposition (1.27–30).

This point is developed, first, in terms of inner unity in the church based upon humility – a point reinforced by the example of Christ whose humiliation was vindicated by God (2.1–13), and, second, in terms of a good witness to the world around them (2.14–18).

Having given this basic instruction, Paul returns to the links between himself and the church, and refers specifically to what may be called the outward occasion of the letter, the impending visit of Timothy (and hopefully also of himself) and the return of Epaphroditus as the bearer of the letter (2.19–30).

In the next section he moves to a fresh topic, that of the danger of rival missionaries who were appealing to Gentile Christians to be circumcised and keep the Jewish law. Woven into this section is a warning against some kind of claim to maturity which was being made by some of the church members and which possibly lay behind some of the divisions in the church (3.1 – 4.1).

Then Paul returns to the question of division in the church, and this time speaks out openly to some of the people who were causing the problems. This merges into some rather general exhortation which is concerned with positive Christian living (4.2–9).

Only after all this does Paul return finally to the work of the gospel and to the help which he had received from the church. It forms a fitting climax to the letter as he expresses his gratitude and prays that God will provide for the needs of the readers who, we may suspect, may have impoverished themselves in their concern for other Christians (4.10–20; cf. II Cor. 8.1–5).

PHILIPPIANS – ONE LETTER OR SEVERAL FRAGMENTS?

A number of commentators have argued that it is difficult to read Philippians as one continuous document. They point to two perplexing passages.

(a) The first is at the beginning of ch. 3 where there is an abrupt shift from 'And now, my friends, I wish you joy in the Lord' in the first part of 3.1 to the strong warning in 3.2 against 'evil workers' and the generally impassioned tone of ch. 3 as a whole. The use of 'And now', which could be translated 'finally', in 3.1 could suggest that the end of a letter was in sight. And the attack on 'evil workers' who have not been mentioned in the earlier part of the letter suggests that a new and different situation is now in mind.

(b) In 4.10–20 Paul offers thanks for a gift sent to him by the Philippians through Epaphroditus. It has seemed strange to some scholars that only at the end of the letter does Paul give thanks in this way for the gift he has received. Would it not be more natural to do so earlier, perhaps in connection with the passage about Epaphroditus visit?

For these reasons it has been proposed that in fact we have parts of two, or more probably three, documents which have been combined to form one letter. One possible division is:

Letter A		4.10–20	
Letter B	1.1 – 3.1;	4.4–7;	4.21–23
Letter C	3.2–21; 4.1–3;	4.8–9	

On this view we have the substance of a letter sent by Paul when he received a gift from the Philippians (Letter A). Then Paul wrote a longer letter dealing with the question of unity in the church (Letter B). Finally, when he heard that a new and dangerous situation had developed in the church, he wrote a further letter to deal specifically with this problem (Letter C). Later, these letters were combined into one. The fullest letter (Letter B) was enlarged by the insertion at suitable points of Letter C (with a slight alteration of order at the end) and Letter A. Whatever introductory and concluding matter was originally present in Letters A and C was dropped.

This decomposition of the letter has not commended itself to most English-speaking scholars. The following points are relevant:

(a) The opening phrase in 3.1 can equally well mean 'furthermore' and is not necessarily a sign of the closing of a letter. The change of subject in 3.1/2 or 3.1a/1b is abrupt but not so abrupt as to be impossible, especially when we bear in mind that letters were not necessarily dictated and written in one continuous session.

(b) The presence of opponents of Paul and his friends in the church has already been hinted at earlier in the letter, and there is a remarkable number of common themes, extending to the use of the same (sometimes unusual) vocabulary between ch. 3 and the earlier chapters.

(c) There is nothing unusual about Paul discussing gifts and money at the end of a letter (cf. I Cor. 16), especially when he has already alluded to the topic in passing earlier (1.5; 2.25), and when the letter is primarily concerned with other matters.

(d) The letter as it stands has a coherent structure which would be lost if it were divided up.

We shall work on the basis that we have one letter in front of us.

Opening greeting
1.1–2

If you were composing a letter at the time when the New Testament was written, there was a set pattern for the beginning, just as is the case today. Letters began (very sensibly) with (1) the name of the writer(s), followed by (2) the name of the reader(s) and then (3) a word of greeting. It is a pattern found with variations in both private and public letters:

(1)   Irenaeus
(2)   to Apollinarius his dearest brother
(3)   many greetings

(1)   From the people of Jerusalem and Judaea, from the Senate and from Judas:
(2)   to Aristobulus, tutor of King Ptolemy and a member of the high-priestly family, and to the Jews in Egypt.
(3)   Greeting and health.   (II Macc. 1.10)

Paul and other Christian writers followed the pattern but they developed some variations on it. First, there was a general 'Christianization' of the form, so that the greeting was used to express the Christian status of the writer and the readers and to offer a specifically Christian wish. Second, there were the individual variations found in different letters.

The writer

1.1a   Except in I and II Thessalonians, *Paul* describes himself in a way that expresses his position as a Christian missionary. He is a *servant of Christ Jesus* (so here; Rom. 1.1; Titus 1.1) or an 'apostle' or even a 'prisoner' (Philemon 1). This title indicates that, although he writes in a very personal fashion, he is conscious of his position. He occupies a humble position as Christ's servant or slave and yet this gives him authority as a Christian leader, and he is writing from that standpoint; this is not just a personal letter from Paul to his friends.

Paul regularly mentions other Christian missionaries alongside himself in the salutation, although he appears to write solely in his own name and person in what follows. Here his colleague is *Timothy* who is also mentioned in every letter written when he was with Paul (I Thess.; II Thess.; II Cor.; Gal.; Philemon). In each case he was known to the recipients through having visited the church, and it may be that Paul also wished to back up his message through the authority of his fellow-missionary. In the present case, Timothy was soon to visit the church.

It is interesting that, although Paul never refers to Timothy as an apostle (cf. II Cor. 1.1), here he places him alongside himself as a servant of Christ Jesus. In this way he indicates to the church that Timothy shared his authority.

The readers

1.1b   The readers are addressed in a way that identifies them as Christians. Here they are are *all God's people at Philippi, who are incorporate in Christ Jesus*. So REB translates what is more literally 'all the holy [ones] in Christ Jesus who are in Philippi'. (Paul can also address his readers as the church(es) in a particular place (Gal.; I Thess.; II Thess.; cf. Philemon); for the combination of both descriptions see I Cor.; cf. II Cor.)

There are three elements in this description:

(a) The readers are given here the name of 'holy [ones]' ((so also in Rom.; Eph.; cf. Col.) This phrase was originally used both of angels and also of the people of Israel. It is here applied to Christians, with the implication that those who believe in God through Jesus, both Jews and Gentiles, are now the people of God. It indicates not only that they belong to God but also that they are (or should be) characterized by the kind of life expected of such people.

(b) The readers are said to be *in Christ*. This phrase (with equivalent forms of expression) occurs some 165 times in the Pauline collection of letters and is plainly of key importance in Paul's theology. There is no agreement among scholars regarding its precise origin and meaning, but a probable view is that it indicates how the existence of believers and their relationships to one another are determined by the fact of Jesus Christ crucified and risen. It can be used, as here, to suggest that a close union exists between believers and Christ. The REB translation *incorporate in Christ Jesus* further suggests that they are formed into one group or community through their relationship with Jesus; thus to speak of Christians being *in Christ* is much the same as saying that they form the 'body' of Christ.

THE USE OF 'IN CHRIST' IN PHILIPPIANS

'In Christ' and equivalent phrases occur 21 times in this letter.

(1) It expresses how God does certain things or gives gifts to his people (2.1; 3.14; 4.7, 13, 19).). Jesus is the channel through which God gives his blessings to his people.

(2) It is used as the normal construction with certain verbs (1.26; 2.5, 19, 24; 3.1, 3; 4.1, 4, 10). These are mostly verbs indicating the object of hope or the basis of confidence and joy. Jesus is the one on whom believers depend and in whom they rejoice.

(3) It characterizes believers as people who have a close relationship to Jesus as a result of which they share in his sufferings and the power of his resurrection life (1.1, 13, 14; 3.9; 4.21).

(4) It qualifies certain types of conduct required of Christians (2.29; 4.2). They are called to behave in particular ways because this is appropriate in a life where Christ is their Lord.

(c) The third phrase describes the readers in their earthly setting – *at Philippi*. Paul addresses *all* of them, and this little word may perhaps be related to the fact of some tension and even quarrelling in the church: Paul excludes nobody from his greeting.

Only in this letter are the church leaders specifically mentioned. The greeting is to the church *with the bishops and deacons*. The word 'deacon' can be used in a very general sense of any Christian workers, including Paul himself (I Cor. 3.5; II Cor. 3.6; 6.4; 11.23; cf. 11.15). It is used in what is apparently a more specific sense in Rom. 16.1 with reference to Phoebe. It seems that a word which could refer to any kind of servant of God in the church came to be used specifically for a particular group of workers. The latter are defined

3

by their position over against another group, the bishops. This is the first mention in Paul's letters of bishops, and the word is not used again in the Pauline letters until we come to I Tim. 3.2 and Titus 1.7, where it appears to represent the leading figures (or the leading figure) in a local church. This usage is confirmed in Acts 20.28 where Paul summons the elders of the church at Ephesus to meet him and in the course of his exhortation addresses them as 'bishops'. Here, then, we have a church 'function' or 'office' (cf. I Tim. 3.1) to which people were appointed by the time of the Pastoral Epistles, and alongside it at the same time we have a group of 'deacons'. 'Bishop' conveys the idea of oversight and pastoral care and 'deacon' that of service, and it is significant that both terms can in effect be used of the same people (e.g. Paul and Timothy both function like bishops but can be called 'deacons'); both elements thus characterize Christian leadership. Nevertheless, there was some division of function in the church and it is likely that those specifically called 'deacons' had less responsible duties than the bishops.

Why are they mentioned here? One possibility is that this was the first Pauline church to have such leaders, and this explains why there was no occasion to write in similar terms in earlier letters. Another view is that they had written to Paul and used these titles to refer to themselves; Paul, somewhat ironically, is content in his reply to speak of Timothy and himself as *servants* of Christ. However, there is no real indication that Paul had a 'thing' against the designations. It is also possible that the leaders of a church were especially liable to persecution, and therefore, in a letter designed to strengthen the church to face opposition, it was natural to refer particularly to them. Perhaps the most plausible possibility is that they are mentioned because they were specifically involved in sending gifts to Paul. But we do not have enough evidence to settle the issue.

The greeting

1.2 The same actual greeting is found word for word in Rom.; I Cor.; II Cor.; Gal.; and Eph. (There is a simpler form in I and II Thess.) It expresses the wish that the two cardinal divine gifts will be with the recipients. *Grace* is the loving favour of God, especially shown towards sinful people, and *peace* is the positive relationship between him and pardoned sinners in which they richly enjoy his blessings. The source of these blessings is twofold: first, there is *God*, who is now known as *our Father*, an expression which is rare (but not unknown) in the OT and was coming into greater use in Judaism, and, second, there is *the Lord Jesus Christ* who is regularly and naturally named alongside the Father as the source of such blessings. Nothing could indicate more clearly how for Paul Jesus stood 'on the divine side of reality' and was linked with God as the origin of salvation.

A Sermon in a Greeting

What points are important for preachers here? Here is a basic description of the church.

(a) The members of the church are those who are 'set apart' as God's people; they are situated 'in Christ'; they need continually to experience divine grace and peace.

(b) The unity of God's people, expressed in the use of *all*; the whole congregation is addressed. The letter is to them all and not just to the leaders. The preacher must love all the members of the congregation.

(c) The need for designated leaders in the church to carry out the two functions of oversight and service; all who so act are the humble servants of Jesus Christ and possess authority for their tasks.

Opening prayer-report
1.3–11

After the greeting it was normal to express good wishes to the recipients of the letter. Christian letter-writers transformed this stereotyped feature into a prayer-report, telling their readers of the things for which they gave thanks to God and/or were petitioning him. Paul follows this practice in all his letters to churches (except in Gal.). He states how he thanks God for the readers (except in II Cor. and Eph. where he blesses God for his gracious acts) and may then move on to a related prayer. The contents of the prayer-report are closely related to the theme of the following parts of the letter. Mentioning the good qualities of the readers in the thanksgiving also serves the purpose of establishing a warm relationship between the writer and the readers which will encourage them to take heed of what follows. It is always a good idea to begin by praising somebody, especially if you are then going on to criticize them!

There is a clear division between the thanks (1.3–8) and the prayer (1.9–11). But the actual flow of thought is difficult to follow, and so it may be helpful to paraphrase the whole section before commenting in greater detail:

> Whenever I pray for you, I make my request to God with joy and I do so because every time I think of you I can do so with thanksgiving to God on account of the way in which you have been my partners in the work of the gospel; at the same time I can make my requests with joy and thanks because I am confident that God will continue the good work which he has begun in you right up to the day of Christ. It is right for me to have this concern for you all because I have great affection for you and because in my bonds and in the defence and confirmation of the gospel I am conscious that you share with me in the grace God gives me. Believe what I say, however extravagant it may seem, for, as God is my witness, I love you deeply with the affection of Christ himself. Here, then,

is what I ask God for when I pray for you. I want your love to develop more and more in knowledge and perception so that when the day of Christ comes you may be sincere and blameless, filled with the fruits of righteousness which come through the work of Christ, and so your life's record will bring glory and praise to God.

Paul gives thanks for the church
(1.3–8)

1.3   Paul implies that he remembers (and therefore prays) frequently about the Christians at Philippi, and when he does so, the feeling that enters his mind is primarily one of thanksgiving to God.

> This at least is the REB rendering. An alternative possibility is that Paul thanks God because the Philippians remember him – not least in the messengers and gifts that they have sent to him. In favour of this view it can be argued that the Greek phrase used normally introduces the cause for thanksgiving rather than the occasion, and that on this interpretation the thanksgiving goes straight to a main theme of the letter, namely what the Philippian church has done for Paul. Against it must be counted the fact that Paul does use similar phrases to this one to express his own remembrance of other people. Either way, it is the character and activity of the Philippian Christians which rouse Paul to thanksgiving.

Paul speaks of *my God* (4.19; Rom. 1.8; I Cor. 1.4; Philem. 4) just as he does of 'my Lord'. He does not mean that God is his God and not anybody else's but that this is the God whom he acknowledges as God and to whom he can confidently address his prayers. The phrase is one that is particularly associated with calling on a divine being or acknowledging him as Lord (3.8 of Christ my Lord; cf. Mark 15.34; John 20.28).

MAKING PRAYER MORE CONCRETE

Praying to God about other people can become something of a vague formality in the Christian church. We tend to pray in general terms for various categories of people ('all doctors and nurses', 'all who are sick') rather than for specific groups and

individuals, and we perhaps fail to thank God specifically for
what he is doing in these people in terms of his gracious purpose.
As we move into the content of this report of Paul's prayer, what
can we learn about the kind of things that we should be saying to
God? How can we make our prayers more thankful and more
specific?

1.4   The congregation at Philippi was such that Paul's prayers for
them were always *joyful*. It was not always so; he was so concerned
about the situation in the Galatian churches that he expressed
neither thanks nor joy at the beginning of the letter, but launched
straight into the attack! But in the present case, whenever Paul came
to pray for the church, his requests were accompanied by joyful
recollection of things for which he could give thanks to God, and
inevitably this gave him greater confidence to make fresh requests to
God.

Joy in Philippians

Joy is one of the key words of this letter, occurring in one form or
another 16 times; in addition, the word 'pride' essentially refers to
joy in what Christ does (1.26; 2.16; 3.3). Joy is a mood of
exultation which is based upon what God is doing in Christ both
in ourselves and in other people (1.18; 2.2, 28; 4.1,10). It is
therefore a mutual activity (2. 17f.) and a feeling that should
characterize the personal relationships of Christians to one
another (2.29). It is something that can be experienced despite
difficult circumstances because of confidence that God's purpose
will triumph. It can therefore face even martyrdom with all its
pain. Yet it can be increased or diminished especially when Paul
considers the progress or lack of progress of his friends (1.4; 2.2).
The joyless Christian is a contradiction in terms; therefore Paul
can call on his friends to rejoice (3.1; 4.4) and expect that growth in
faith will be accompanied by growth in joy (1.25).

The concentration of words for joy in this letter is remarkable. In
particular the emphatic repetition of the command to rejoice (2.18;
3.1; 4.4) must have some specific grounds. It seems that the
experiences of the church, coupled with its knowledge of Paul's
imprisonment, must have introduced a pessimistic feeling into it.
There was grumbling and there was depression, and the spirit of
dissension will have contributed to this. Paul's remedy for the

situation is, in part at least, to encourage the readers to take fresh heart and to realize that God's intention for his people is that they should be filled with joy.

1.5 The *part you have taken in the work of the gospel* may be the basis for Paul's thanksgiving or for his joy; the distinction hardly matters. Here Paul is thinking of something distinctive about this church both in character and in extent. Another of the major key-words of the letter lies behind this expression, *koinonia*, often translated as 'fellowship', 'communion' or 'participation'.

FELLOWSHIP IN PHILIPPIANS

This word was used to describe the situation where two or more people have something in common, for example, when they are partners sharing in a common business concern or when they share in the proceeds. Two main nuances of meaning thus arise. On the one hand, the stress may be on the way in which the partners are brought into a relationship with one another through their common activity, and on the other hand, the stress may be more on the way in which each participates or shares in the particular activity or benefit.

The idea is found in this letter in 1.5, 7; 2.1; 3.10; 4.14, 15. Paul uses it to express how Christians share together in the grace of God which enables them to do their work in proclaiming the gospel (1.7). They also share together in the Holy Spirit (2.1), and because of this there is a common bond between them, so that Paul can urge them to live together in harmony and unity. Christians also share together in the suffering and afflictions that arise out of opposition to the gospel (1.7; 4.14). Finally, Christians share with one another their material resources, and in particular the Philippians helped Paul in this way during his missionary work even after he had moved on to other towns (1.5; 4.14 and 15). It is through their common participation in the work and the grace of God that Christians are bound together in partnership and love.

Paul also uses the phrase to speak of his own personal fellowship with the sufferings of Christ (3.10; cf. I Peter 4.13).

More than other Pauline letters Philippians indicates the importance of Christians sharing together in the work of the gospel through being conscious of what they can do to supply the needs of others and then getting on and doing it. We tend to place 'the great apostle Paul' on a pedestal; he was very subject to human weakness and relied immensely on the prayers and help of all kinds of his friends in the different churches. Christian workers today are no different in their need for support and fellowship.

In the present verse it is clear that Paul and his readers are the two partners. But in what do they share? The object is simply stated as *the gospel*. This could refer to their sharing in the blessings conveyed by the Christian message, summed up as 'salvation'.

Alternatively, it could refer to their sharing in the task of spreading the gospel, and this is the sense adopted in the REB translation. There can be little doubt that the latter view is on the right lines, as is confirmed by what Paul says later in 4.15f.

However, these later verses suggest a more specific sense is present here. They indicate that the sharing in the work of the gospel was expressed in the financial help which the Philippian Christians gave to Paul 'in the early days' of his mission and which they were now repeating. The coincidence with the language used here (*from the first day until now*) demonstrates that the same thought is in mind.

This may make us wonder whether the word *koinonia* here should not be understood in the sense of a concrete 'contribution' or the quality of 'generosity'. However, this is probably unjustified, and it is preferable to think of the sharing between the Philippians and Paul in the work of evangelism with special reference to the financial help that they were giving him and to the way in which they had sent Epaphroditus to help him.

It should not need comment that what impressed Paul was not just the fact of this help but the way in which it had continued and shown fresh expression despite a period when it had not been possible. II Cor. 8.1f. indicates some of the difficulties under which the church had laboured.

1.6 At this point Paul encourages his friends by declaring his certainty that God is going to continue to work in their lives.

A major problem in this verse is how it is tied to its context. REB fudges the issue by starting a new sentence at this point without indicating its logical relationship to what precedes. Silva takes the verse to give a further reason for the joyful sense of gratitude. Our suggestion is that it gives a further reason why Paul offers his prayers of intercession for the church with confidence and joy – because he has grounds for believing that they will be answered, based on his trust in the purpose of God.

Again we come to a characteristic word of this letter, *confidence* (1.14, 25; 2.24; 3.3f.). Paul expresses his certain hope that various things will happen – a confidence that is based not on human or worldly considerations (the language of rational weighing of probabilities; 3.3f.) but on his conviction that God will work out his plan of salvation and provide whatever means are needed to that end. Therefore he was sure that he himself would be able to visit the church again for its spiritual welfare (2.24). His colleagues where he was imprisoned had gained a confidence from his imprisonment to proclaim the gospel with greater daring (1.14). In 1.25 he expresses his confident belief that it is more important that he remain alive to help the readers and on the basis of this belief he can say that he *knows* that he will remain with them. In general, then, confidence is based on knowledge of God and his loving power to achieve his plans. Hence here Paul can express certainty that God will complete his work in the lives of the readers. There is the implicit argument that it is unthinkable that God will break off what he has already begun to do.

But to what is Paul referring when he speaks of *the good work* that God has begun?

This phrase is not found elsewhere of something that God does, and so does not appear to have a fixed reference. Commentators have suggested:

(1). The work of 'creation', described as 'good' in Gen. 1.

(2). The work of salvation beginning with their conversion, by which the readers are made more and more the kind of people that God wants them to be.

(3). The work of evangelism, in which the readers were sharing with Paul.

This last possibility is attractive because the preceding and following verses both speak of the way in which the Philippians were sharing in evangelism and in the grace given to evangelists. But Paul's language elsewhere about completing the Christian life (II Cor. 7.1; Gal. 3.3) and the content of his prayer in 1.9–11 suggest that the wider thought of Christian growth is in mind.

The sharing by the Philippians in the work of the gospel was one – very significant – expression of the fact that God was doing his work in their lives. Verse 7 then gives further evidence of this specific fact, and in vv. 9–11 Paul then prays in a more general way for their spiritual growth.

It thus emerges that a concern for the work of evangelism is a sign of the spiritual life which God implants in Christians. Further, growth in maturity is an essential aspect of the Christian life. Such growth is dependent upon the grace of God. We shall find throughout this letter the paradox of Christian growth being ascribed both to the activity of God and to the effort of the Christians themselves. One might compare how people cannot work physically unless they take in the food provided for them; this picture suggests that the last word is in our hands in that we can choose whether or not to eat and so to be nourished for our work; but here the picture breaks down because it is clear that God as it were often 'feeds' us independently of our own efforts.

Paul relates this process of growth to what he calls *the day of Christ Jesus*. This phrase and its equivalents (1.10; 2.16; cf. Rom. 13.12; I Cor. 1.8; 3.13; 5.5; II Cor. 1.14; I Thess. 5.2, 4; II Thess. 1.10; 2.2) always refers to the future time when Christ will come as judge and saviour. It is modelled on the OT concept of the 'day of the Lord'. It is significant that, since Christ takes over the function of judgment on behalf of God the Father, so the coming day becomes the 'day of Christ'. The phrase *bring it to completion by the day of Christ Jesus* is more literally 'will go on completing it until the day of Christ Jesus'. Paul envisages the possibility that his readers will survive until the coming of Christ and that God will go on working in their lives until he comes. The point then, is not so much the completion of the task or the complete perfecting of the readers as rather the fact that God will continue his work in their lives right to the end and not abandon them at any point.

THE NEARNESS OF THE DAY OF THE LORD

The thought that Christ may come during our lifetime is one that has become unreal for many Christians. Equally, the thought of a catastrophic end to the world is remote. Many early Christians doubtless expected that the coming of Christ could take place within a very short period of time, but by the time of this letter Paul had certainly come to reckon with the possibility of his own death and even of martyrdom before the day of Christ. The realization of this did not cause any major change in his outlook, and he was able to frame his remarks so as to be applicable whether or not people survived until that day.

But what are we to make of this concept of a 'day of judgment'?

At the very least we can say that to speak of a day of judgment is to declare our commitment to the existence and the importance of moral values, our determination to live by them and our condemnation of behaviour, including our own, that falls below them. More specifically we are stating that Christ, as we know him from the NT, is the criterion of these moral values.

The Christian who believes that Jesus died and rose again, however, must surely go beyond this. The resurrection, with its affirmation of a life that conquers physical death, is the basis for the conviction that Christ continues to be active and will consummate the work of salvation which he began. It is inconsistent to affirm the resurrection of Jesus and yet to deny the reality of his activity in the next world. And it is surely also inconsistent to affirm a resurrection which somehow shatters the course of ordinary history and to deny that history can be shattered again by the coming of Christ in a new way. It is dangerous to take the resurrection seriously! There is thus a dimension of future judgment woven into the fabric of a Christian belief which takes the resurrection seriously. If Christ is the beginning, Christ too must be the ending.

1.7   One of the difficulties with modern translations of the NT is that they very properly break down the rather long sentences to which writers of Greek are prone, making the various clauses into shorter sentences; unfortunately in so doing they often do not indicate the logical relation of the clauses to each other. Here there is no break with the previous verse and the connecting 'as' has been omitted. The thought appears to be that Paul offers thankful and joyful prayers for his readers just as it is *only natural* for him to *feel like this,* i.e. think in this way (cf. 3.15) or perhaps 'be concerned' (cf. 4.10) about all of them (cf. II Thess. 1.3).

THE CHRISTIAN MIND

Yet another key-word of the letter is used here, the verb 'to think' (2.2a, 2b, 5; 3.15a, 15b, 19; 4.2, 10a, 10b). Probably unconsciously Paul indicates the importance of thinking in a Christian manner; the mind and heart of the believer should be moulded in a characteristically Christian way. Paul's usage brings out three ways in which this should happen:

(a) Christians must think in a certain way (2.5), have a

13

Christian frame of mind (3.15a), rather than think in a different
way (3.15b) and be concerned for earthly things (3.19). This
suggests that our minds can form definite patterns of thinking (cf.
how we may be attuned to approach a particular topic from the
angle of a conservative or a socialist and find it difficult to escape
from this mind-set). The Christian must cultivate a Christian
mind-set.

(b) They must think in the same way as other Christians and
have a common mind (2.2a, 2b; 4.2); this is another way of
expressing the need for Christian unity. How does this relate to
independence of thought and freedom to criticize within a
Christian group?

(c) They should think of people with loving concern (4.10a,
10b); the quality of love should affect our thoughts as well as our
actions.

It is natural for Paul to have this concern for his readers for two
reasons. The first is that he has *great affection* (1.7) for them all.

This is the probable sense of a Greek phrase which might also mean
'because you have great affection for me' (cf. NEB; Hawthorne; the Greek
word-order strongly favours the REB).

The second is that he is conscious that when he is *in prison* and has
to *defend the truth of the gospel* all of the readers share with him in what
REB calls *this privilege of mine*. A number of points stand out here.

The first is that Paul is linked to the readers by strong ties of
affection; a Christian group which does not begin to experience a
growing love for other Christians is lacking something that Paul
would have regarded as essential.

Second, Paul again emphasizes that he is thinking of all the
readers. No matter how much disunity there was in the church Paul
held them all in affection and regarded them all as his partners.

Third, Paul regards the readers as sharing with him in his *privilege*,
literally 'my grace'. Although 'grace' can refer to the totality of God's
loving attitude and his gifts to his people, in the present context with
its reference to the work of the gospel it is much more likely that Paul
is thinking of the particular grace which fortifies the witnesses to the
gospel in their work (Rom. 12.3, 6; 15.15; I Cor. 3.10; Gal. 2.9). What
is important is that, although Paul speaks elsewhere of the grace
given to him personally, which might suggest that he was thinking
of a special endowment for apostles, here he is saying that all the

readers share with him in this gift; nobody is excluded in principle. Had Paul never heard of the difference between the ordained ministry and the laity? Obviously not.

But of course this leads to the fourth point to note which is that Paul saw his friends at Philippi as engaged in the same task of witness. He is thinking primarily of his own situation (*while I am kept in prison*) and his own activity, in which the readers obviously could not share; but the implication is that in their sympathetic support for him – by sending Epaphroditus and their monetary gift – they were sharing as far as they could in his need and his task as a witness. Thus, although he says that they share in grace, he implies that they share in the situation in which grace is needed.

1.8 *God knows how* might suggest that there was some doubt about the sincerity of what Paul has just said and that therefore he needs to call on God to witness to the truth of his statement. But there is no indication that the readers did doubt what he was saying, and therefore it is more likely that Paul is simply stressing as strongly as he can the depth of his feeling for them; it is more a case perhaps of 'Only God knows how much I long for you.' Perhaps the strong asseveration is required because Paul goes on to claim quite boldly that he has *the deep yearning of Christ Jesus himself* for them.

LOVE IN THE CHURCH

The whole passage is an object lesson on the mutual affection of a missionary and the congregation. It is expressed most powerfully in this letter, but it is also present in other Pauline letters (cf. Rom. 1.9–12 to a church which he had not founded; I Cor. 4.14; II Cor. 2.3f.; Gal. 4.19; I Thess. 2.8).

Paul's prayer for the church
1.9–11

1.9 At last Paul gets down to the content of the petition which he offers for the readers. It is not a prayer that they might have love or that their love may increase, but rather that their *love may grow ever richer in knowledge and insight of every kind.* Paul is not saying that knowledge is absent from their love, but rather that it is needed to an even greater extent. The implication is that love may not be accompanied by knowledge. Love can be insufficient by itself since it can be directed towards the wrong objects or it can treat the objects of its affection in inappropriate ways: a parent's love for a child, for example, can be over-protective or selfish. Even if we agree that true love seeks the best for the object of its love, and that therefore love has to include an element of knowledge and insight, our love may still not be all that it ought to be because it doesn't know what is best for the loved one.

But what precisely has Paul in mind here? The trouble is that he writes in very general terms, and one could be forgiven for suggesting that he is simply using pious phraseology as a substitute for clear, sharp thinking. Can we clear him of this charge? Is he thinking of love for God or love for other people or both? The next verse may help us.

1.10   The result of knowledge is expressed as *enabling you to learn by experience what things really matter.* This phrase (also found in Rom. 2.18) conveys the idea of a person testing things to see whether they measure up to a standard and approving those which pass the test, and hence REB interprets it of a process where by repeated testing of different things a person comes to know and recognize the kind which will pass the test. The things that pass the test thus stand out as those which are best (NRSV) or which stand out from others and so *really matter.* The Christian, therefore, is called to exercise discrimination.

JUDGMENT AND DISCERNMENT

We are sometimes told that Christians should not judge other people, and there is a sense in which it is wrong to be condemnatory of others, especially without examining sufficiently carefully the reasons why people do wrong things. But there is no future for the person who lacks discrimination and the moral sense to know what is approved by God and to practise it. Whether these are things to do or things to take pleasure in is not clear. If we cast a glance at the occurrence of the same phrase in Rom. 2.18, there it comes in a discussion about Jews who know God's will and are taught from the law. They therefore consider

Paul's prayer for the church 1.9–11

themselves competent to teach and guide others. It looks, therefore, as if we are concerned with making the right moral choices in
life and guiding others in right behaviour. Parents with the wrong
sense of values will not be good guides to their children. So the
thought seems to be that love for others will be accompanied by
right behaviour and setting a good example that others can follow.

That it is God's standards which are in mind here, as in Rom. 2, is
clear from the next phrase which refers to the successful outcome of
such discrimination. The readers will be *flawless and without blame* on
the day of judgment. The first of these words meant 'sincere' or
'pure', denoting a character free from blemish. The other word can
refer both to being blameless oneself and also to being harmless to
other people. Since appearing at the judgment is in mind, REB has
rightly adopted the former rendering. Paul's longing is that, when
measured by God's standards, his readers will not be found faulty.
The judgment is carried out by Christ rather than directly by God. It
is a common thought in the NT that the judgment which is the
prerogative of God inasmuch as he is God and supreme is carried out
on his behalf by Christ – a fact which has important implications for
the high status attributed to Christ by his followers. We should note
that Paul appears to be thinking of the present condition of his
readers and not of some special transformation that will take place in
the future. The idea is that whenever the day of Christ comes the
readers will be ready for it rather than that the day itself will work
some transformation in them. No doubt Paul expected some time to
intervene before that event so that the readers would have time for
growth in the qualities that he desired to see in them.

1.11   Paul now describes the character that he wants to see in a
different way. The readers are to yield *the full harvest of righteousness*.
They are to be like plants which bear a healthy crop of fruit, and this
fruit consists in righteousness (or possibly springs from their
character as justified or righteous people). We note that Paul cannot
conceive of a Christian way of life which does not have moral
effects. Righteousness in the OT and NT alike is expressed in social
justice and fair dealing. Paul could thus be thinking of a purely
human quality brought about by human effort. But he says that the
harvest is made possible *through Jesus Chris*. How this happens is not
spelled out here, but we shall not go far wrong if we remember that
for Paul believers are brought into a life of close union with Jesus in

which his character is reproduced in them. When this happens, the motivating and energizing power comes from Jesus himself (or is the effect of the working of the Spirit of God who is also the Spirit of Christ). At the same time, however, Paul may be thinking of the way in which Jews thought that they could be righteous through performing the works required by the law of Moses and thus establish their own righteous status before God (cf. 3.6). Already Paul wants to exclude that possibility by insisting that the Christian's righteousness – both in status and action – comes from Christ and not from the law or human effort of which a person might boast. He therefore finally insists that if Christians do show the harvest of righteousness it brings fresh *glory and praise* to God. People will praise God for what his people do, and the effect is to enhance his greatness and repute.

The Paradox of Grace

We meet here a frequently expressed paradox of the Christian life. The Christian growth of the readers is dependent upon Christ. It is also dependent upon the prayers of a person like Paul; he believes that his prayers do effect changes in those for whom he prays. That might appear to suggest that the readers will be carried along willy-nilly to Christian perfection by God's power. It might also raise questions about the possibility of spiritual growth and progress for people who are unfortunate enough not to have a Paul praying for them. But on the other hand, it is abundantly clear that believers in Philippi and elsewhere do not always make the progress that they should, and also that they are called to spiritual effort.

How these factors are related to one another is not clear. We might compare how the moral and intellectual growth of a child is dependent both upon the help provided by parents and teachers and upon personal effort, and we cannot neatly isolate the inputs from either side and say which is decisive. Paul cannot produce a model of the divine-human situation which is any clearer than this human situation which leaves so many questions unanswered. But, just as no parents worth their salt would leave it all to their children (or try to do it all for them), so too Christians believe that God and other Christians play their part in their spiritual progress and thankfully acknowledge it. Nor do they assume that it is all being done for them, and they therefore need to do nothing themselves. See also on 2.12.

Paul's own situation and prospects
1.12–26

From a prayer which was largely concerned with the spiritual progress of the readers themselves, Paul proceeds to a section which is mainly about himself and his own situation.

It seems entirely natural that in a communication to people who had not heard for some time what had happened to him (remember the slow speed of ancient communications, slower even than some mail today!) Paul should move into a report about his own situation without further ado. He regarded his readers, indeed, as partners in his witness (1.7). He deals with his situation in terms of its significance for himself but also bearing in mind how it affects his readers. The conclusion which he reaches is that what has happened has turned out for good, and that he will be able to continue to help them to grow in their Christian faith.

Nevertheless, commentators have a penchant for discovering subtleties in what can be understood in a straightforward manner. The subtlety detected by some is that Paul goes at length into his own situation especially *vis à vis* the people who are trying to annoy him in order indirectly to say something to the readers about the party spirit among themselves. Certainly they could apply something of what Paul says to themselves, but then virtually anything that Paul says can be applied to the readers of his letters, whether he deliberately intended it to be so or not. We may wonder whether the assumption that Paul is *primarily* concerned to give deliberate indirect exhortation is justified here.

What then does Paul say?

(1) His imprisonment has turned out to be for the promotion of mission rather than the reverse (as his readers might have feared).

(2) This is so, even though some people are preaching the gospel from wrong motives. Paul will not let this get him down.

(3) This whole event will lead to his 'salvation' as a result of the prayers of his partners. Christ will be glorified whether he lives or dies.

19

(4)   For himself Paul would almost prefer to depart and be with Christ, but he has the conviction that he will continue to live and help his readers – and in particular that he will visit them.

We can now see that Paul is in effect explaining why he cannot be with his readers at the present time, and why, therefore, a letter has to do instead. In this letter he will give them the instruction which he would have delivered orally had it been possible to do so.

The positive effects of Paul's imprisonment
1.12–14

1.12   When Paul addresses his readers by some such phrase as *my friends* (1.12), it is often a sign that he is beginning a new section of his letter, and this is obviously the case here. Literally he writes 'brothers', a word used for people joined together by family or other close ties. Jews referred to fellow-Jews by this word, and Christians also used it among themselves (cf. 3.1, 13, 17; 4.1, 8, 21). *What has happened* to Paul is, of course, his imprisonment and its effects. The readers, having heard of it, could well have thought that it would hinder the work of Paul. He believed that it had *actually* been helpful to *the progress of the gospel*. Here the 'gospel' means the work of proclaiming the gospel, the task of evangelization.

1.13   Paul now explains more precisely how his imprisonment has furthered the progress of the gospel. There are two ways in which this has happened. The first is that what has happened to him has become widely known in two areas. The narrower area is *throughout the imperial guard*.

> Here REB has, probably correctly, identified the Gk. *praitorion* as the body of soldiers known as the praetorian guard; these were a regiment of crack troops based in a military campsite just outside Rome. The REB footnote gives another possible translation of the word: it could also refer to a place where a military governor resided, hence 'the Residency', such as could be found in Caesarea, but not, it seems, in Ephesus (which was the capital of a province with a civil governor).

The broader area is *among the public at large* (literally 'all the rest') and is quite vague. Paul is thus saying that he has become known amongst the military establishment in the place where he was imprisoned and to a wider circle of people who had dealings with the prisoners. He is probably not thinking of Christian believers in Rome: they already knew about his imprisonment.

It was not of course the fact that Paul was a prisoner which had become known, but rather that his imprisonment was *in Christ's cause*.

> Here REB is attempting to get the sense of the difficult phrase 'in Christ' (1.1) which is here used in an unusual manner of a thing (Paul's imprisonment) rather than of persons. Paul can only mean that his imprisonment was because of his commitment to Christ and to the gospel rather than for any of the usual reasons (such as falling into debt or awaiting trial for some criminal offence).

But how had this happened? We can safely assume that questions could well be asked about a person brought to prison on an unusual charge and that gossip would quickly spread among the guards. But we can probably also assume that Paul himself must have taken the opportunities to speak to people with whom he came in contact, especially since he goes on to imply that his example has spurred on others to Christian witness.

1.14   This indeed was the second result of his imprisonment. It had encouraged *most of our fellow-Christians* to speak out boldly. Paul probably implies that they had been doing so to a certain extent, but now they were doing so all the more. Their boldness had two roots. On the one hand, the occasion of it was seeing Paul's behaviour. A good example can nerve us to do things that we formerly felt too frightened to do. If one boy jumps the stream, the more timid ones will follow. On the other hand, Paul appears to mean that his own boldness encouraged the others to have *confidence* in the Lord and so to increase in courage and to speak out without fear. They did not mind what consequences might follow, when they saw that Paul was even prepared for imprisonment and whatever might follow it.

> The statement might also mean that 'many of the brothers in the Lord' had gained confidence as a result of Paul's imprisonment.

Here, then, we have an expression of Paul's continual concern for the task of evangelism. He measured the value of whatever he did or whatever happened to him in terms of whether it helped on this work. Even apparent setbacks could still be used as occasions for witness. And Paul is obviously glad that the other Christians around him were taking up the task. The implication is that evangelism was not just the task of a few selected Christian leaders. It was something that the majority of Christians could and did undertake. But they were human, they shrank back from the possible consequences, and they needed something that would help them to trust more fully in the Lord so as to free them from timidity.

Two kinds of evangelist
1.15–18a

1.15–16 At this point the story takes a slightly surprising turn. What Paul has just said needs some qualification. There were in fact two groups of people carrying on evangelism in the vicinity of Paul. One group was acting out of *a jealous and quarrelsome spirit*. The other group was motivated by *goodwill*. Paul then further characterizes the two groups in reverse order. The former group acted out of *selfish ambition*; they preached Christ *from mixed motives* and especially from the motive of causing Paul *distress*. The latter group acted out of *love*, in the knowledge that Paul's imprisonment was concerned with the defence of the gospel.

We can understand this latter group quite easily. They are allies of Paul, motivated by goodwill toward him, and indeed, more than that, by love for him. They know that his imprisonment is because of the task of evangelism, and they are committed to that task and want to do all that they can to forward it, precisely in order to make up for what Paul as a prisoner cannot do. This, then, is a fuller description of the people whose activities Paul regarded as contributing to the progress of the work of the gospel.

But what about the former group? Who were they and what exactly were they doing? The basic point that Paul makes is that their preaching took place from wrong motives and was intended to irritate him. They were preaching Christ, but if their preaching was meant to irritate him, there must have been something about it that was not quite right. It therefore seems likely that their message had elements in it which were not wholly acceptable to Paul. The people in question were preaching Christ, and therefore they were not unbelievers, whether Jewish or Gentile.

Commentators generally assume that they were either Judaizing Christians who advocated some measure of obedience to Jewish beliefs and practices or else they were Christians of a more Pauline sort who were envious of Paul's success and were trying to undermine his influence. Neither view is free from difficulty. The problem with the former view is that usually Paul is much more vehemently opposed to such people, comments on their errors and regards them as enemies of the gospel. The difficulty with the latter view is to identify more precisely a convincing scenario. Nevertheless, it is quite within the range of possibility that there could be evangelists who were anxious to establish themselves over against Paul and who may have objected to his position of eminence in the church.

On the whole I tend to favour the latter view. Paul refuses to be irked by what is going on, and it is difficult to believe that he could have viewed Judaising with such equanimity whereas he might not have been so troubled by people who were preaching the truth even if they had ulterior motives for doing so.

A WORD TO PREACHERS

It is related that when Dr F. B. Meyer was experiencing great popularity as a preacher in London, Dr G. Campbell Morgan came to Westminster Chapel, and the fickle sermon-tasters switched their affections in large numbers; it required (and found) considerable grace in the older man to acknowledge the greater popularity of the younger man and to thank God for him. Similarly, Paul had to reckon with the devotion of some of the Corinthian Christians to Apollos instead of himself. In neither of these cases, to be sure, was there the desire to irritate the other preacher, but it is not too difficult to envisage a situation where a preacher or evangelist is not free of the desire for self-advancement and even of the desire to do better than somebody else and to cause them feelings of resentment. Indeed, are any of us wholly free from such motives on occasion?

It is conceivable that one reason why Paul mentions these things is because of the situation in Philippi. The mention of 'selfish ambition' as a failing of the Philippians in 2.3 encourages this view. If so, the point remains implicit rather than explicit, and Paul does not take it up specifically.

1.18a Rather he is concerned with commenting on the significance of the situation as far as he personally is concerned. What is the outcome of it? Only this one thing, that Christ is being proclaimed. Paul's concern is solely with the effects on evangelism. And the fact is that one way or another people are hearing about Jesus. That is what matters to Paul. To be sure, some of the preaching is happening *sincerely* and some otherwise. The contrast appears to be between pure and false motives. No doubt it is not a good thing in the end of the day if the evangelists have wrong motives and their primary concern is, for example, to be able to count converts to their own credit instead of giving the glory to God (and it is possible to claim to be giving the glory to God when really we are claiming some of that glory for ourselves because God is doing it through *our* activity). But perhaps it is better that Christ be proclaimed from the wrong motives than not at all, and Paul makes it clear that instead of being irritated by this attempt to make him feel envious he will rather rejoice in the successful outcome of the evangelism. Any attempt to 'get him down' is doomed to failure. Paul's joy is not to be quashed in this way.

Paul's confidence for the future
1.18b–20

1.18b But now he moves on to the wider situation concerning himself, and the REB wisely begins a new paragraph to indicate this shift in theme. The new thought is closely connected with what precedes by repetition of the thought of rejoicing. Paul will *go on rejoicing* in respect of the total situation. The keynote of the letter (1.4) keeps recurring.

1.19 Paul's joy stems from the fact that he has confidence (*I know well* expresses here a firm conviction) that the whole state of affairs – not just the rivalry of some Christians but his imprisonment and the risk of worse to come – will issue in what is here called *deliverance* (literally, 'salvation'). This 'deliverance' might be meant literally of being set free from prison, but this is very unlikely because Paul goes on to refer in this selfsame sentence to what will happen *whether the verdict be life or death*. We should rather understand 'deliverance' in a spiritual sense of the development of Paul's spiritual life and his attainment of what God intends for him (cf. 1.28; 2.12; and the description of Christ as the coming Saviour in 3.20; Paul's phrase echoes Job 13.16). Let us bear in mind the temptations that Paul was conscious of – sheer frustration at being confined, irritation and envy with those who were taking advantage of his being out of the way, abandonment of hope in the face of physical privation, giving up his faith and Christian profession under threat of legal penalties including execution. There was strong temptation then to lead Paul to spiritual ruin. But he is confident that he will not succumb to it but will rather attain to salvation (cf. II Tim. 4.18).

Paul's confidence is based on two factors. The one is the continuing prayers of his friends; Paul writes as though his own personal adherence to the faith depended on them. Nothing could indicate more clearly his conviction that God acts in response to prayer; people who have nobody to pray for them appear to be spiritually vulnerable. This is a thought that we may not altogether like: surely, we say, God cares even for those who are so lonely in the world that they have nobody to pray for them. And yet on the other hand, this thought does not hold us back from praying especially for our family and our friends in the belief that it does make a difference to them. Somehow we have to hold together these two beliefs, that God cares for those who have no earthly helpers and that our prayers move him to care for others.

Second, Paul is dependent on *the Spirit of Jesus Christ given ... for support*. The implication is that this is what is given to Paul when his friends pray for him. The language probably implies that the Spirit was given to him in a generous, abundant fashion by God. Paul could mean that the Spirit was given to him as a means of support and strength or that the Spirit provides him with support. In view of what Paul says in Gal. 3.5 about God providing the Spirit, the former is more likely (so REB). Paul may be thinking of the promise of the Spirit coming to help believers to bear a faithful witness when they are persecuted (Mark 13.11), but the thought is probably much broader than this.

1.20   In the next verse Paul repeats in different words the substance of his conviction about the future. He expresses a *confident hope*, literally an 'eager expectation and hope'; the REB translation brings out the element of confidence and certainty well, but it misses out on the element of eager longing for the hope to be fulfilled. We find the same element in Rom. 8.19.

The content of the hope is that *nothing will daunt me or prevent me from speaking boldly.* Here REB is interpreting a phrase which is literally 'in nothing shall I be ashamed but in all confidence' and taking it to refer specifically and only to Paul's courage in speaking out as a Christian. In other words, Paul is expressing his confidence that he will not display shame at being a Christian but will rather bear a bold witness (cf. Rom. 1.16). Another possibility is that Paul means that he will not be put to shame in the way that one feels utter public embarrassment when one's hopes are not fulfilled. The contrast which Paul goes on to express with what Christ will do in him supports the first of these two interpretations, but with the qualification that the REB limitation to 'speaking' boldly is too narrow; what Paul means is that he is confident that through the help of the Spirit he will not be tempted to be ashamed of Christ whether in speaking as a Christian in court or elsewhere or in suffering as a Christian if it comes to the point of martyrdom. He is sure that he will not let Christ down but will rather be able to speak and act and suffer with *boldness.*

Just as has happened *always* so far, so *now* in the immediate future *Christ will display his greatness in me.* I am not too happy with this translation, and prefer to render it 'Christ will be glorified in me'; that is to say, whatever Paul says or does will have the effect of bringing glory to Christ and so making him appear great rather than of casting shame upon Christ, and it seems to be this thought of Paul acting so as to show the greatness of Christ rather than the thought of Christ displaying his great power in protecting Paul which is present here. What Paul is thinking primarily of is what will happen in his own body (REB: *in me*), with specific reference to the possibility of his continuing life in that body or of his death as a martyr in that same body. Paul is thus concerned on a very down-to-earth level with what is going to happen to him. He is looking at the alternatives in absolutely realistic terms. He will go on to explain more fully how Christ will be 'made great' in either situation and why either possibility is something to which he can joyfully look forward.

But what stands out is the tremendous confidence expressed that he will continue to serve Christ faithfully. The conviction that the Spirit of God will give him all the strength that he needs is obviously powerful and suggests that Paul had spiritual experiences of a very direct sort which convinced him of the power of God at work in his life.

Life and death with Christ
1.21–26

1.21 This verse explains how it is that whether he lives or dies Paul will not be put to shame and Christ will be glorified in him. The explanation lies in the fact that in both cases Christ is the centre of his existence.

For Paul living means simply *Christ*. This has been understood in two ways. First, it might seem that here Paul is thinking of what life means to him: what is his aim in life, what is it that thrills him? The answer is that the longer he lives the more opportunity there will be for Christ to show his greatness in him.

The difficulty with this view is that it seems to suggest that Christ shows his greatness for the benefit and enjoyment of Paul, whereas previously the point was that Christ was being displayed to the world. We are therefore compelled to the alternative view, namely that what Paul is thinking of is the fact that life means serving Christ, since for him life has no other meaning.

The truth is that in this paragraph Paul is scarcely able to distinguish the two ideas of serving Christ and knowing Christ, the latter being an experience which brings untold joy to the person concerned. But for Paul knowing and serving Christ cannot be separated from one another. The accent then is on life as a means of serving Christ – which is enjoyment of Christ.

But then when he says that death is gain, the thought is undeniably of gain for Paul himself who will thereby come into closer knowledge of Christ. The remainder of the paragraph makes it clear that this is the general sense. Life now is opportunity for service; death is thought of, not in terms of martyrdom as a means of serving Christ, but as the route to a deeper experience of Christ.

1.22 Paul now looks more closely at the two possibilities. He has just said that death is gain. But there is a counterbalancing factor. If he is allowed to continue living in the body, then he has the opportunity for *fruitful work*. He can go on with his work as a Christian missionary, and he believes that this work will produce results. It may be that Paul is thinking here of the possibility of continuing to serve Christ and thus continuing to please him by the work which he does. He may well also be thinking of the fact that fruitful labour means that he will have something to show for his labours at the day of judgment and will thus gain the approval of his Lord. However, this is not actually said here (contrast I Thess. 2.19f.), and we may be wrong to read this thought into the passage. It does look as though Paul is thinking simply of the opportunity of serving Christ – an activity in which he takes delight.

Thus there is a choice between the 'gain' of death and the opportunities in life. It is not surprising that Paul asks which possibility he is to choose (supposing that he were free to choose), and confesses that he cannot make up his mind. The language is rhetorical and does not imply that Paul had the freedom to choose. He might pray to the Lord for one or the other, just as he prayed for the removal of the 'thorn in his flesh', but in the end the matter was entirely in the hands of the Lord.

1.23   The next two verses spell out the choice more fully by indicating the factors that are relevant and bringing out as sharply as possible the acute tension that existed in Paul's mind as he faced the two possibilities. *I am pulled two ways* gets the point with all desirable clarity. Paul feels like the rope in a tug o' war contest. First, there is his own *desire*, a longing to *depart and be with Christ*. The word *depart* arouses such pictures as an army breaking camp and leaving the site, or a ship casting off the ropes and leaving the harbour. The word conveys forcefully the sense of a complete break or separation, and it is not surprising that it became a synonym for dying in the sense of setting off from this life and moving somewhere else. For Paul this new destination was to *be with Christ*.

> Some commentators have connected this hope with death by martyrdom, seeing it as the especial reward for martyrs. But this is unnecessary. There is no need to think of this goal as being one that was preserved for those who died as Christian martyrs. It would be surprising in any case if the concept of martyrdom had developed to such an extent by this early date. Nothing in fact suggests that so exclusive a thought is in Paul's mind.

How does this thought relate to that of the coming of Christ at the End (cf. 3.20f.) and of the resurrection of the dead to be with the Lord? Paul, in other words, appears at first sight in I Thess. 4 and I Cor. 15 to imply that the dead are not united 'with Christ' until the End. However, he does also speak of those who 'die in the Lord' (I Thess. 4.16). The picture in that letter in fact seems to suggest that dead believers are with the Lord, so that when he comes from heaven he will bring them with him. It is true that in the same passage Paul also speaks of the dead being resurrected and then they and those still alive are caught up to meet the Lord in the air. It looks as though Paul is struggling with ideas that cannot be expressed with one set of images. By the time he wrote II Corinthians, which is earlier than this letter, he was clearly of the opinion that the dead were absent from the body and with the Lord (II Cor. 5.8). The resurrection of the body is associated with the coming of the Lord at the End. Paul must have conceived of a soul or other centre of personal existence which somehow continues in being even when separated from the body. Existence apart from the body was not something desirable in itself (if that is how II Cor. 5 is to be understood), but the fact that it brought a person closer to the Lord did make it desirable. This is what Paul has in mind here. Paul does not develop this point and the associated problems here. The thought of being with Christ is paramount for him. And he is clear that it is better than life in the body with all its attendant pains and temptations.

Nevertheless, this is not what Paul would choose for himself. From his own purely personal point of view there is no doubt what is better. But that is not the decisive consideration. Remaining *in the body* with all its attendant hardships and its imperfections is *the greater need* when Paul considers the situation of his readers (and other people to whom he felt the same obligation). There was work to be done in helping them in their Christian faith and in spreading the gospel among a wider circle. It was not that Paul necessarily considered himself indispensable and thought that nobody else could do what he was doing. Nor, as we have noted, was the choice in his hands. But if he had the power to decide, then he would have to say that present Christian service was more necessary than personal enjoyment of full communion with Christ in the world to come.

SALVATION OR SERVICE?

One is reminded of Moses in the story in Exodus. He was willing to be blotted out of God's book if only this would compensate for the sin of Israel when they made the golden calf and worshipped it (Ex. 32.31f.). And was it not Wilberforce who said that he had no time to think about his own soul, so occupied was he with caring for the needy? It is not easy to reach the level of Christian love for others which can ignore the concerns of oneself. And while it is arguable that people cannot truly love others for Christ's sake if they have not tasted from the wells of salvation and if they are not continually sustained by their communion with Christ, there is a temptation to Christians to put their own spiritual growth before showing love to others. But is it not also true that the path to spiritual growth and to knowledge of Christ may be through self-sacrificing love? And is not Christ himself the pattern of the selfless life that leads to God?

There is, of course, the way of life which is supremely activist and is expressed solely in the service of other people. It is clear that this is not what Paul has in mind as one of the alternatives. There are people who scorn the vertical dimension of life and insist that the horizontal is what matters. But for Paul there is a genuine tension between the development of his own personal relationship with Christ and his concern for other people that they also may come to know Christ. In short, Paul's concern for other people is that they may know that fulness of life (in both dimensions) which comes from knowing Christ, and it is precisely because he knows how wonderful the experience of salvation is that he is prepared to sacrifice his own enjoyment of it in order to help other people to enjoy it. One might compare how a husband and wife will have to cut down the amount of time which they spend purely in each other's company in order to care for their new baby; they do so in order that the young child may grow up to enjoy the fulness of life which they have, and of course they find that they experience new joys as husband and wife together in parenthood.

1.25   But the fact that a person is sure that a particular path is the best one does not necessarily mean that it will open up. Paul could have been sure that he was very much needed by the church and yet God could have ruled otherwise. According to the REB Paul was able to say that, because he has come to this settled conviction that he was needed by the churches, he was therefore *sure* that he would remain alive and continue his work.

It is also possible to translate: 'And I am absolutely convinced of this, namely that I shall remain and stand by you all.' In that case the ground for Paul's certainty is not stated, and we are left to assume that it rested on some way in which he became sure that this was God's will for him (cf. Rom. 14.14, where his certainty rests 'in the Lord Jesus'). But even on the

REB translation there is a jump from 'I am sure that this is the more necessary' to 'I am sure that this will happen', and we have to posit that somehow Paul knew that his reasoning was at one with God's judgment in the situation.

Paul's certainty, then, was that he would *remain and stand by* his friends. The former verb indicates his continuation in life in the body, and the latter his presence with his friends to sustain them and help them. As a result he believed that he would see their *progress and joy in the faith*. Just as the work of mission can show progress (1.12), so too can the faith of the individual. Faith develops by becoming stronger and more exclusively rooted in Christ, so that the believer stands all the more firm in the midst of temptation and hardship. Faith also gives rise to joy as the believer achieves a deeper relationship with Jesus Christ and sees the spread of the gospel. Faith is intended to be a joyful experience (Rom. 15.13), not a cause of misery. It is true that faith will lead to hardship and even to persecution which could well tempt the believer to despair and gloom, and it would be quite unrealistic not to acknowledge this fact. Many believers have had and do have to live in much harsher circumstances than would have been or would be the case if they were not believers. Yet with faith comes a joy that triumphs over human afflictions.

1.26 When believers experience this growth in their faith, they have all the more *cause for pride in Christ Jesus*. The fact that leads to this pride at Philippi is that Paul is once again able to come to them – and to come in order to help them to grow in their faith. They are therefore joyful in respect of him and his coming because of what this means spiritually to them. REB refers to their *pride in Christ Jesus*. 'Pride' is perhaps not the best translation because human pride and arrogance is continually condemned in the Bible. It is difficult to separate pride from selfish feelings of one kind or another. Here, however, it is 'pride in Christ Jesus' which is at issue. Believers can be proud of what he has done for them. But it would be better to avoid all scope for misunderstanding by translating the Greek word as 'exultation', which means that happiness which accompanies acclaiming the greatness and goodness of somebody else. There can be a genuine happiness and rejoicing at what somebody else is doing, and the believer can feel this towards Christ and what he is doing for us. There is thus an ineradicable personal element in it – we

31

rejoice because of our involvement with Christ and because we benefit from what he does for us – but it is free from any kind of arrogance or self-satisfaction or feeling of human merit.

DEATH AND THE CHRISTIAN

This is undoubtedly one of the most significant discussions of the nature of Christian existence in the face of death in the NT. The points emphasized here are basic and need no translation for the present day. But it is important to bring out the Christian character of what is said and to contrast it with ordinary human attitudes to our situation and with purely nominal Christian attitudes. It is easy to take a fatalistic attitude of 'whatever happens is for the best' which is thoroughly passive, whereas the attitude of Paul here is very positive. He has a genuine desire for both of the eventualities which presented themselves to him. He would be happy to go to be with Christ; he would also be happy to remain at his work. He saw the two possibilities as 'good' and 'better' rather than as a choice between the greater and the lesser evil or as purely neutral.

Paul's attitude might well seem to be an unacceptable one for Christians today. He appears to positively welcome the thought of dying and thereby could give the impression of regarding the present life as of no significance in itself. Better to die and enjoy the benefits of life after death with Jesus. Such an attitude appears to be world-denying. It seems to represent an unhealthy and morbid preoccupation with death which is quite inappropriate for people today. It may be all right for people living in wretched surroundings, plagued by chronic ill-health and physical debility and denied all possibility of enjoyment in this world, but not for the majority of people. How can we possibly take over Paul's attitude?

Two main points can be made.

The first is that Paul is not primarily comparing this world and the next. He is asserting that the knowledge of Christ which we will have in the next world is even better than that which we now have. He is comparing a good thing with something even better. That is not necessarily a world-denying attitude.

The second point is that Paul is very much concerned positively with this world. He considers the service of other people to be so important that he willingly puts aside his own desire for a closer knowledge of Christ in favour of serving Christ right here in this world. He was concerned that people should come together and enjoy all the richness and fulness of the new life in community in Christ here and now. Later on in the letter he expresses the wish that the readers will focus their minds on 'all that is noble, all that is just and pure, all that is lovable and attractive, whatever is excellent and admirable' (4.8), and nothing suggests that he narrowly circumscribed the extent of such things. In short, the new life in Christ is concerned with the renewal of creation, and what happens in the church now is the re-creation of human society to be what it ought to be. Life in this world takes on positive direction because it is filled with the promise of what God can make of human life rather than being a losing battle against the things that make life miserable and wretched.

We can go further and emphasize the positive points which Paul is making. He reminds us that our existence is not bound by this world. We have to face death squarely and what lies beyond it. And for Paul there is something that lies beyond it. Paul is fairly silent about what happens to unbelievers, but he has plenty to say about the joy of life with Christ. There is a powerful inducement to Christian faith not merely in its offer of freedom from condemnation but also and above all in its offer of full salvation.

It follows that our life in this world is not the ultimate thing. We must not overvalue this world and our achievements in it. There is another perspective. Life in Christ remains the supreme good. From this perspective we can recognize the danger of a life which fails even to get the best out of life in this world because it ignores the spiritual dimension which gives life its fulness in the world.

Consequently, the most important thing that we can do is to promote the anticipation of life in the next world right here in this world. There is no dichotomy between saving people from their sins so that they may be able to enjoy the presence of God in eternity and saving people from their sins so that they may live the new life in the Spirit here and now. These two aims are one.

Appeal for unity and humility in the church
1.27–2.18

It has become apparent that, although the preceding section began with a discussion of Paul's own personal situation, the underlying theme was 'the progress of the gospel', which included 'the progress of the gospel in Philippi' and Paul's own share in promoting it. Consequently, the section ended with the thought of spiritual progress in the church at Philippi. This gives a smooth transition into the next section which is concerned with the immediate problem in the church, namely the lack of unity which was perhaps the principal barrier to spiritual progress. 1.27 accordingly gives the key-thought for this section – a life worthy of the gospel and specifically one of unity in the church. In 1.28–30 this is developed in terms of the need for fearlessness in the face of opposition and the consequent possibility of suffering. This is followed in 2.1–4 by a renewed appeal for the avoidance of rivalry and disputes. In 2.5–11 the career of Jesus is powerfully presented both as that of an example to be followed and as that of a Lord to whom obedience is due. This then leads to a renewed appeal to the readers to avoid grumbling and dissension and rather to demonstrate their obedience by shining as lights in the world. All this combines to make a massive appeal for Christian love and unity for its own sake and also for the sake of the effect on the outside world (2.12–18).

Unity and opposition
1.27–30

1.27 *Whatever happens* probably refers specifically to the situation of Paul himself. The one thing that the readers have to do, regardless of the outcome of the matters he has been discussing, is to live in the right kind of way. There is the possibility that Paul may be set at liberty quite soon and be able to visit them; equally there is the possibility that (whether at liberty or otherwise) he may have to be content simply to receive news about them. But that should make no difference to the situation. Either way their Christian duty is plain, and whether Paul sees them or hears about them, the news should be the same. The wording probably suggests that Paul was not sure that his visit would take place immediately.

How then are they to live? The word *conduct* refers literally to the sort of life expected of people as citizens in the community to which they belong, and thus conveys the idea of fulfilling one's social obligations. The metaphor is a living one; it recurs in 3.20 and is used by other ancient writers. Paul is thinking here of how Christian conduct should show itself in the Christian community. Basically it should be *worthy of the gospel*. The Christian message implies a certain way of life and provides a standard by which Christians can assess themselves. Elsewhere Paul can speak of living in a way that is worthy of the God who has called them (I Thess. 2.12), but here he refers to the gospel message in which this way of life is described. Pre-eminently it is a life characterized by a rich love for the other members of the group. Paul develops the idea with three phrases.

(1) First the readers must *stand firm, united in spirit and in mind*. The two ideas contained here are manifestly of firm resistance to anything that could move them and of unity within the congregation.

It is a matter of debate whether here *spirit* should be taken as referring to the Spirit as in Eph. 4.4 where it is the agent of unity in the church. The fact that *mind* is named here in the same breath rather speaks against this interpretation.

UNITY IN THE CHURCH

Two points can be made at the outset which underline the relevance of this passage. The first is that Paul is here concerned with unity within a specific congregation. Nowadays the word 'unity' tends to be associated with relationships between Christians in different denominations, and the problem is to encourage them to love one another despite differences in doctrine and practice and in this context of love to try to understand and overcome these differences. What Paul says here can be applied to that situation, but he is primarily concerned with love within a congregation, and there is surely a case that this is where Christian unity must begin.

35

The second point is that perhaps the greatest problems in a congregation are not due to doctrine or Christian practice but rather to faulty personal relationships, to jealousies and bickering of various kinds. Consequently, this section speaks directly to what is a major problem in many a congregation. Here is fundamental teaching that every congregation needs. It is to our shame that people no longer look at High St. Methodist Church and say 'See how these Christians love one another' (as outsiders said of the early church, according to Tertullian).

Paul is implying that a group of people cannot remain strong as a group if they are not of one mind, if different people have different ideas of the group's goals and if they are not bound together by mutual affection and care. It is also true that specific individuals will not stand firm in allegiance to the group if they do not share the same goals and feel a sense of commitment to the other members. But here it is probably the viability of the group as a whole that is in Paul's mind. The group can be whittled away as first one member and then another, or one small sub-group and then another cease to cohere with the others. Behind Paul's concern lies the consciousness that the group was threatened by people who were trying to destroy it. The Christian church must never cease to be vigilant and must never assume that the opposition has disappeared. There may be moments when the attack is stronger than at other times, and there may be times of advance and growth, but these things always happen in the context of a struggle. Christians are battling to paddle up a river against the pull of a stream which is stronger in the rapids than in other places where it flows more leisurely through flat countryside, but the stream is always moving inexorably downwards, and if the oarsmen ship their oars, the boat will inevitably lose way and begin to drift with the stream.

Secondly, Paul exhorts his readers to contend *side by side in the struggle to advance the gospel faith* (cf. 4.3). Again there is the same thought of a united stand against opposition, but now there are two fresh thoughts. If the previous phrase was about standing one's ground, this one is about active participation in a struggle or contest. It is probably correct to say that here the mood has shifted slightly from defence to attack, from maintaining a position to making an advance.

The REB translation indicates rightly that what is at issue is the kind of faith demanded by the gospel, faith in Christ. This faith is almost personified as a person engaged in the struggle or in need of allies to defend him and promote his cause. It is not clear whether the reference is to the readers promoting their own faith and the associated way of life or to their evangelistic efforts to lead others to faith. There could be the thought that the gospel message and its requirements are being compromised by pressures on the church and that its purity must be preserved. In the context the thought of preserving the purity of the gospel, which is in danger of being compromised by an unworthy lifestyle, is perhaps uppermost.

ONWARD, CHRISTIAN SOLDIERS ?

The martial imagery about 'marching as to war' has a basis here. All who abhor violence (including, but not confined to pacifists) may dislike the use of 'war' imagery, and there are some who even dislike any element of 'competition' and 'contest' in human relationships. Nevertheless, it is impossible to think of existence in this world without being conscious of evil as an opposing force which knows no such scruples and without engaging in a struggle which is forced upon us. The victory is the victory of good over evil; since the aim of evil is to destroy goodness, good wins precisely by refusing to be anything other than good, in other words by rejecting the tools and methods of evil. Thus the language of struggle and of war can be used without suggesting that any approval is given to violence. In this way we can justify Paul's language in the church today. We can and must contend for the *gospel faith* by using the weapons of righteousness (II Cor. 6.7).

1.28   The third element in the catalogue is *meeting your opponents without so much as a tremor*. Now the underlying reason for Paul's concern comes to light. The readers are under pressure from other people who are described as 'opponents'. If Paul uses the language of war on occasion, he also can recognize certain people as adversaries who are hostile to the gospel. Of course Christians are called to love their enemies, but this command is not to be reinterpreted to mean that they should not or cannot have any enemies; on the contrary, they are to recognize that there are people whose aims are hostile to them and the existence of the church, and that their activities are to be resisted. Love for enemies must not blind us to the necessity to resist evil.

Who are these opponents? There are two possibilities. The first is that they are non-Christians outside the church who are making life unpleasant for Christians in an attempt to make them give up their Christian faith. The situation is one of persecution. This is the generally accepted interpretation.

A second possibility is that Paul has in mind the kind of people who professed the Christian faith but who held a version of it very different from his and who propagated it forcefully in the churches which he had founded. On this view the truth of the gospel was equally in jeopardy from people who insisted on forcing Judaizing practices on Gentile converts – circumcision, Jewish festivals and food laws – and who were thus denying that faith in Christ was sufficient for salvation.

In favour of the former view is the fact that when the word is used elsewhere in the NT it generally refers to people outside the Christian faith (Luke 13.17; 21.15; I Cor. 16.9; II Thess. 2.4; I Tim. 5.14). The presence of such adversaries is perhaps to be seen in 2.16 and of course in references to Paul's own imprisonment. In favour of the latter view is the extended discussion of such adversaries in ch. 3. Further, the strong language used here by Paul is of a piece with his stern words about rival missionaries in II Cor. 10–13 and Galatians.

The language used is indeed strong. Paul says that the steadfast demeanour of the readers is *a sure sign to* their adversaries *that destruction is in store for them and salvation for the* church. Here he is undoubtedly thinking of the outcome of the final judgment as exclusion from eternal life or full entry into it. The opponents ought to recognize that the readers' perseverance in their faith is something acknowledged and vindicated by God. The strong language is paralleled elsewhere. We shall find it again in 3.19. It is used of opponents of the faith in II Thess. 1.6–9; those who are not believers are described generally as 'those who are perishing' in I Cor. 1.18. But it is paralleled in what Paul says of his opponents in the church in II Cor. 11.15; Gal. 1.8f. It therefore seems quite possible that in this verse Paul could be thinking of the dangerous inroads made by rival missionaries, but it must be admitted that certainty is impossible.

Either way, we should note that Paul is not here threatening his opponents with destruction, but pointing out that they should recognize in the calm demeanour of the readers an indication that they are on the wrong path. This is *a sign from God himself*, a sign that can be ignored or otherwise interpreted.

1.29   A new idea is introduced at this point. The readers could easily have been tempted to believe that their present situation of opposition and adversity was a sign that they were not on the road to salvation – especially if they were being attacked by Judaizing Christians who insisted that they were not doing everything that was necessary for salvation. Paul therefore insists that they must not be frightened or distressed by opposition, *for* (emphatic!) the sign that they are God's people is that they have been chosen not only to believe but also to suffer for Christ. The important idea which is expressed here is that the suffering of Christians is a sign that they belong to God; they have taken his side in the struggle against evil, and therefore it is not surprising if they have to take their share of the attacks which are directed against him. We have the same thought in Rom. 8.36 where Paul uses the words of Ps. 44.22 to indicate that when Christians suffer persecution it is for God's sake and cannot therefore be something that separates them from him or from his love (cf. also II Cor. 4.11). On the contrary, it is regarded as a *privilege*, as something that God has graciously granted to them.

How can this be the case? It is obviously not that suffering is regarded as a good thing or an enjoyable experience. Rather Paul is saying that the readers have been enabled not only to believe in Christ – and this is regarded as something conferred by God – but also to have the privilege of suffering on his behalf. This is evidently something that goes beyond just believing. The point is that they have been called into the service of God – which is a privilege – and this includes the possibility, indeed the likelihood, that they will have to suffer because the work of God always rouses opposition from evil and the opposition takes the form of painful attacks. Such pain is borne *for Christ*; just as he suffered for Christians, so they now suffer for him. Paul would no doubt say that, if Christians remembered how much Christ suffered for them to deliver them from sin, surely they would count it a privilege to take their share of suffering on his behalf in helping to promote his reign in the world.

There are occasions when we can regard suffering and hardship almost as a privilege. If somebody whom we particularly love or respect is in great need, we may well be happy to undergo some sacrifice or hardship or even pain in order to help them. The task involves some kind of unpleasant experience, and it would be wrong to say that we enjoy it, but we bear it with cheerfulness and even with joy because we know that we are suffering it instead of somebody else or in order to help that person, and that consciousness helps us to accept what would otherwise be a burden and discomfort. Paul is applying that kind of perspective to the sufferings that Christians undergo for the sake of Christ.

1.30 The final point which he makes is that through their share in suffering they are enrolled in the same conflict as he is in. They had seen his sufferings in Philippi – we may think of the attacks by the people of Philippi at the time the church was founded, or continuing persecution which is not otherwise recorded (or think of the threats that led Paul to travel to Syria via Macedonia in Acts 20.3), or perhaps the bitter attacks of rival missionaries – and they had heard of his situation in prison. What they were now undergoing in threat and reality was no different and in a sense bound them the more closely to Paul. There was no difference between the apostle and the church; if they shared together in the work of the gospel (1.5, 7), they also shared equally in bearing the sufferings involved in that work. Paul doubtless intended this fact to be a means of encouragement to them. Writing to the Corinthians, he could suggest ironically that the church got all the benefits while the apostles bore all the suffering (I Cor. 4.8–13) but this was addressed to a church that shrank away from suffering and foolishly imagined that Christians were exempt from it. In fact the church must be as apostolic as the original apostles, and for Paul it is of the essence of apostleship that it involves suffering for the sake of the gospel and the Lord. Therefore, we do the gospel a disservice if we somehow convey the impression that all there is to being a Christian is simply believing ('Come to Jesus and be happy') and do not face people realistically with the stern demands and the call to commitment and readiness for whatever may be demanded of us. It must, of course, be reiterated that this is not a call to masochism, to the desire to suffer and to the enjoyment of suffering as suffering; that is a perversion of what Paul says.

Love in the church

2.1–4

2.1 Verses 1–4 are a repetition and reinforcement of the command that the readers should live and work together in unity (1.27). The actual command comes in vv. 2–4 and develops new aspects of what unity means in the life of the church. The purpose of v. 1 is to supply a fresh motive for the command. The opening *If* is not meant to cast any doubt on the reality of the existence of what belongs to *our common life in Christ*. Rather the force is: 'If, as is indeed the case, our common life in Christ...', and Paul's intention is to make the readers realize that *if* certain things are true in their lives, *then* the logical consequence is that they should behave in a certain way.

Four statements are made about the nature of the Christian life which are true in the experience of the readers. All of them have to do with their *common life*. They are various aspects of God's working in the inner lives of believers and in their life together which he conveys through Jesus Christ to whom they are 'joined' spiritually. He is the source and channel through which divine blessings and commands come to us, and therefore it is true both that we experience them only through our 'life in Christ' and that such a life should be inevitably accompanied by them. If we are not experiencing them, individually and as a Christian group, it may be a moment for self-examination to ask whether we are really sharing to the full in life in Christ or have drawn back from too close a contact with him.

(a) *Anything to stir the heart* represents a Greek word that can have the sense of 'comfort' or of 'exhortation'. Either of these incentives can indeed stir the heart, whether to rouse it from despondency to joy or from sluggishness to action, but probably it is the latter that Paul has in mind. Paul is suggesting that if the readers are 'in Christ' then this situation contains a certain forceful appeal to them to which they should be responsive. He is their Lord who urges and encourages them to do what is right.

(b) *Any consolation of love* means 'any incentive that arises from the fact that you are loved'. Here the stress probably lies on the divine love experienced by the readers; it should fill them with an answering love and a willingness to obey the divine commands. It may be that this phrase should be regarded as a closer definition of the previous one, in which case the force of the exhortation lies in the love experienced by the readers. People will do things out of love

41

that they wouldn't do out of any other motive, and the test of the reality of love is whether we are willing to please the beloved.

The word translated 'consolation' has more the sense of 'encouragement, incentive, persuasion'.

(c) *Any participation in the Spirit*

This is a tricky phrase. Literally it is 'any communion/sharing of the Spirit', and it is the same phrase as that which appears in the apostolic blessing in II Cor. 13 where it is translated 'the fellowship of the Holy Spirit'. This more literal translation was probably preserved here in the REB because of the stereotyped use of the words in Christian meetings, and it is a more helpful starting point in determining what Paul means. The phrase can refer to:
  (1) a fellowship among believers created by the Spirit;
  (2) a participation by several people in the Spirit; or
  (3) a fellowship between believers and the Spirit.
We can probably rule out the last of these. The first interpretation has its defenders, who take the phrase to refer to a unity among believers created by the work of the Spirit. But it is a strong objection to this view that there does not seem to be any parallel for the use of 'a fellowship of X' to mean 'a fellowship created by X'. The fact that Paul can talk in a very similar way of a participation 'in the life of his Son Jesus Christ' (I Cor. 1.9) suggests that the same kind of thought is present here. In other words, at this point the ruling idea is the way in which believers experience various divine powers, including the power of the Spirit. Thus the REB translation here 'participation in the Spirit' is to be preferred.

The Spirit is the source of spiritual life, love and power, and therefore those who participate in the Spirit have the power at their disposal to live as God wants them to do.

(d) *Any warmth of affection or compassion* refers to the kind of love shown by Jesus himself (1.8) and then displayed by Paul to the readers. When people are joined together in Christ, then they come to have the kind of love that Christ had for them. Somehow the experience of being loved by God (Rom. 5.5) fills us with love, just as the knowledge that somebody loves us can trigger off an answering love in our hearts.

INCENTIVES TO CHRISTIAN UNITY

The effect of these four phrases is to make the point that when people are in union with Christ, they should experience a sense of overwhelming obligation in view of the love shown to them by

42

God and of the experience of participating in the life of God. Paul has shown that we have:

(1) a command to obey;

(2) an encouragement to obey that command;

(3) the power of the Spirit to enable us to do so; and

(4) the quality of love to fulfil the command spontaneously and joyfully.

2.2. Now Paul comes to the point of application. If the readers individually and collectively have this remarkable experience of God, then the obligation lies upon them to live in a particular way in relation to one another. A relationship with God carries with it consequences for life with one another in the congregation of believers (cf. I John 4.11).

These consequences are basically expressed in terms of how the readers are to behave towards one another, but Paul puts this indirectly because he wants to pull in another motive for their conduct. If they are concerned to make him feel happy – as they ought to be in view of the close bonds between them – then they will live in harmony with one another. What Paul could have said was 'Think and feel alike – and as a result you will make me happy', but he preferred to put it the other way round: 'Make me happy by thinking and feeling alike.' He makes it appear that the result of their common life in Christ should be to make him joyful, and they will achieve this by living in harmony among themselves.

KEEPING THE CHURCH LEADERS HAPPY

Paul's personal appeal is worth noting for congregations today. Would we automatically think that one of our duties is to make our pastor or church leaders happy and joyful by the quality of our Christian lives? Do we want a pastor to say when he leaves us, 'I am grateful that you tried to make me happy by becoming the kind of congregation that God wants you to be'? Hebrews 13.17 contains a similar instruction for us.

It might seem fair to draw the inference from the phrase *fill up my cup* that Paul already felt a sense of joy with regard to the readers (as indeed he has already said in 1.4), and that what he is asking for is the icing on the cake, the 'extra' that will make his joy all the greater. Yet it would be wrong to draw the conclusion that what he desires is an optional extra. It is clear from the letter that harmony and love between believers is of the essence of Christian conduct.

Paul supplies no less than four phrases in this verse to give examples of what is involved (and there will be more to follow!).

(1) *Thinking alike* is literally 'thinking the same thing'. When the congregation consider what they are to do or what attitudes they are to have, then they should all come to the same conclusion.

(2) *Feeling alike* (this is presumably the translation of Greek *sympsychoi,* literally 'united in spirit') suggests that the readers are to be united in feeling as well as in thought. What seems to be meant is the sharing of the same attitudes.

(3) *With the same love for one another* obviously means that everybody is to show the same quality, namely Christian love.

(4) *With… a common attitude of mind* is literally 'thinking the one thing' and is almost a repetition of the first phrase. It perhaps suggests that the readers should have the same, single goal.

UNITY AND DIVERSITY IN THE CONGREGATION

Preachers may be tempted to try to find subtle differences between the qualities in these four phrases, but it may be better to take them together. We have here the rhetorical device of piling up synonymous phrases to heighten the effect. But we can nevertheless suggest that they indicate that the readers should have:

a common way of thinking (a Christian mind)

a common set of emotions (the readiness to rejoice with those who rejoice and to weep with those who weep)

a common love for one another, and

a common set of goals for the group.

One might object that there is a danger of forcing the readers into a common mould, so as to be people who react in precisely the same way, mere clones of one another with no minds of their own, possibly even people who are ready to do without question whatever the leaders of the congregation suggest. It should be clear that this is not Paul's intention. He is arguing that where the life of the church is concerned, the readers should try to achieve unity in their thinking and goals; individuals should subordinate their own ideas of what is best and especially any selfish desires to the mind of the group as a whole and seek its good. It is perfectly possible for people to think independently and creatively in harmony with one another. It should equally be possible for them to have genuine differences of opinion as to the right way to proceed and yet to come to one mind in the end.

2.3 If the instructions in v. 2 were rather general, Paul now spells out with greater precision what he means. The negative and positive sides of having unity in the church are expressed in turn. Two attitudes are to be shunned, namely *selfish ambition and vanity*.

We have already come across the first of these in 1.17. One of the effects of that verse should have been to invoke the sympathy of the readers for Paul himself as the victim of such an attitude on the part of other people. Now he warns against the danger of the same attitude among the readers. It is the kind of motive which tries to promote self-interest at the cost of other people, the desire for superiority and the position to boss other people.

The second phrase is found only here, but a related phrase is found in Gal. 5.26, again with reference to an unhelpful attitude in the church. *Vanity* is the motive which leads people to do those things on the basis of which they can boast or hope to receive the applause of others. There may well be things that we can do which rightly merit applause, but the Greek word used here conveys the sense that the pride is 'empty' in that the achievements are not worth boasting about.

The positive counterpart to Paul's negative instruction is to *humbly reckon others better than yourselves*. Paul cannot mean (for example) that expert musicians should consider bungling learners better at music than themselves. He does mean that they should not consider themselves as qualified to receive preferential treatment over against learners or as being better or more important people than them. In fact they should consider the other people as *better* – and therefore treat them with the appropriate respect and love.

2.4 Paul is, to be sure, not saying that we should have no concerns or ambitions of our own. The readers are not to think just of their own interests; they are also to take into account those of other people (cf. Rom. 15.1–3). It now becomes clear that what Paul condemns in verse 3 is things that we do to boost our own ego or to score off other people and show our superiority to them. Even our own 'rights' must sometimes be put second.

HUMILITY AND SERVICE

This is revolutionary stuff. In a shipwreck the sailors might well say 'women and children first' in allotting places in the lifeboats, but there are not many other situations where they would say naturally that the women and the children are 'better' than themselves. Parental love may be willing to die for the sake of saving the children from a burning house, but we don't think that our children are more important than we are when it comes to the question of whether they can have the lounge or sitting room to play games when we want to entertain our friends.

But if Paul doesn't mean that kind of thing, what does he mean? Is not the thought that, when we think we deserve preferential treatment because of our status in society or when we think that our opinions are worth more than those of other people, we have to be prepared to put ourselves second?

It would be illogical to suggest that people should be concerned only for the good of other people, since that would mean that our own good could be advanced only by other people doing things for us and not by our own efforts. That line of thought could lead to the ridiculous situation experienced by the students in some missionary training colleges of a former day, where they were forbidden to help themselves to anything on the meal table, but had to wait for somebody else to offer it to them; inevitably a good deal of kicking legs under the table and other more subtle types of hint were practised!

Again, it would be wrong not to encourage people to have a proper self-respect and to do things of which they can properly be proud; it is better, for example, for a child to do well in school and enjoy the pleasure of attaining good grades rather than to perform in a mediocre fashion. But it is surely wrong to boast about one's success and, above all, to look down on other, less successful people.

Paul, then, is not condemning the cultivation of those things which are for our own good. But in thinking about them we must not become self-centred and allow our own interests to blind us to the needs of others. The point needs to be made because it is human nature to see our own interests and needs much more clearly than those of other people. It is rare to find a pressure group which is not concerned to some extent with its own interests, however much it may plead the common good of society. Selfishness is innate in the human personality. The Christian should be concerned to help other people to attain what is good for them. Just as parents may put much effort into helping a child to develop a particular gift – and may do so at the cost of promoting their own gifts – so too Christian believers will do their best to help other people to attain their goals and to inspire them to do things that they scarcely thought possible for themselves.

The example and lordship of Christ
2.5–11

This section clearly forms a self-contained unit. Paul is still discussing the question of the attitude that Christians should adopt in relation to one another, but in vv. 6–11 (which follow on closely from v. 5) the discussion widens out and we have a description of the career of Jesus which at first sight seems to be developed for its own sake and to go beyond the immediate point at issue.

Commentators have often asked whether Phil. 2.6–11 is based on an existing Christian 'hymn'. Because of the apparently independent nature of the material in these verses it has often been argued that they were composed prior to the writing of the letter and then inserted here. They form, on this theory, a statement about the career of Jesus with the purpose of expressing a Christian understanding of him and showing why it is that he is to be confessed as Lord.

Moreover, commentators have noted the rather careful, balanced structure of the clauses at this point which is expressed in some translations (though not in REB) by printing the passage as poetry (see GNB, NIV and NRSV for example).

The unusual character of the thought and the wording used to express it have further suggested that the passage may not have been composed originally by Paul but by somebody else (REB encloses the passage in quotation marks, as if Paul was quoting from another source).

And, to press even further in speculation, there are some indications that the passage could have been originally composed in Aramaic.

We have, then, on this view an early Christian 'hymn', in the sense of a semi-poetic confession and celebration of the lordship of Jesus which may have been sung or chanted or recited in unison by a group of early Christians. The task of the commentator is then widened out, for it becomes necessary to explain the significance of this hymn not only in its present position in the letter but also in its original context.

Although this is an attractive and widely supported theory, there is reason to be somewhat sceptical of various aspects of it.

To begin with, while the passage has a more stylized, formal character than the surrounding material, there is really no agreement among commentators as to how it is to be divided up into poetic lines. To make such an analysis work most practitioners have to allow that some words were added by Paul, and here again there is no agreement on how to separate the original from the Pauline additions. This does not mean that there is not necessarily a correct way of doing it among the various options that have been offered, but it inclines us to caution. It may well be better to understand the section as an exalted kind of prose rather than as poetry.

Then, from the example of I Cor. 13 we know that Paul himself could write in this formal style.

Further, as we shall try to show, the passage does fit into its context rather too well to suggest that it has been adapted from another source. There are important parallels with what is said in ch. 3, and, while this could mean that Paul was inspired by the hymn to adopt its language later in the letter, it is equally plausible, if not more likely, that the ideas expressed in both places flow from his own mind.

Finally, what is said about Jesus here fits in with what Paul says about him elsewhere (though never so fully and systematically as here).

For these reasons it can be argued just as strongly that Paul is certainly using pre-formed ideas about Jesus here, but that it was he who put them together and framed them in such a way as to serve his purpose here in this letter.

There has been also much dispute over the origin of the ideas in the hymn. One widely held view is that the dominant motif is a comparison between the earthly Jesus and Adam and the different choices which they made (cf. Rom. 5.12–21; I Cor. 15.21f., 45–49). While this motif may well be present, in our opinion it is more likely that the hymn is using ideas based on the concept of Wisdom, who went out from her dwelling place with God to be with mankind.

2.5 The opening verse is one of the most tricky in the letter. *Take to heart among yourselves what you find in Christ Jesus* expresses the probable meaning. Paul has been writing about how the readers are to think and the attitudes which they are to have amongst themselves in the congregation. *Take to heart* repeats a verb which he has already used twice in v. 2 and expresses yet again the need to have the right attitudes in their relationships with one another. *Among yourselves* indicates that Paul is thinking of their attitudes towards one another that come to expression in how they treat one another.

But how are they to behave? According to *what you find in Christ Jesus*. I take this to mean that they are to observe how Jesus behaved and to follow his example (GNB, NIV and NRSV take the same line). What Paul has done already is to tell them how to think (and so to behave) as Christians in view of God's provision for them (vv. 1–4); now he tells them that there is a further (and absolutely compelling) reason for so doing, and it lies in a consideration of Jesus Christ and how he acted.

An alternative possibility which is popular with commentators is that Paul means something like 'Think in your relationships with one another in the same way as [you {ought to} think] in Christ Jesus.' That is to say, there is a certain kind of attitude which should develop for people who are 'in Christ Jesus', whether because they have been brought into close union with him and share his way of thinking, or because they live their lives in the new situation where he is their crucified and risen Lord, and therefore they are determined by his authority and his example.

The thoughts expressed in this interpretation are helpful and appropriate, but it is very difficult to make the Greek sentence yield this meaning, and the simpler understanding in REB is preferable.

2.6   It is important to note the structure of the whole statement about Christ. It has two main parts, vv. 6–8 in which Christ himself is the subject, and vv. 9–11 in which God is the subject. The first part, then, is about Jesus and his attitude and actions. It has the logical structure:

[Although]
> *he was in the form of God,*

[nevertheless]
> *he laid no claim to equality with God,*

but
> [he] *made himself nothing,*
> *assuming the form of a slave.*

[And]
> *Bearing the human likeness,*
> *sharing the human lot,*
> *he humbled himself,*
> *and was obedient, even to the point of death,*
> *death on a cross.*

This outline shows that we are told a fact about Jesus which might have led to a certain course of action which he did not follow. Instead he did something quite different, and this is then explained in detail in a series of parallel phrases.

The starting point, then, is that *he was in the form of God.* Immediately we are confronted with a paradoxical statement. 'He' must refer to 'Christ Jesus'. If Paul is thinking about the time before Jesus was born, we must understand him to mean 'The person who was to be born as a man and known as Christ Jesus was [originally] in the form of God.'

> The verb translated 'was' indicates an existing state; we could almost translate 'was originally'.

However, there is another possibility. The first man, Adam, was created in the image and likeness of God (Gen. 1.26), and it is possible that Paul is simply saying that, when he was born, Jesus (like Adam) was made in the image of God. This is certainly a possible understanding of this part of the passage, but we shall have to consider whether it does justice to it as a whole.

Already, however, we have discovered in effect two understandings of *the form of God.* On the one hand, it could describe a person who shared in the essential character of God, who had whatever is involved in being like God rather than being like a human being, an angel or any other kind of being. (The word 'form' is perhaps not the best translation, because in English it tends to convey the idea of a shape which is outward and visible and which does not necessarily correspond to the inner reality.)

On the other hand, it could refer to the way in which human beings (as opposed to animals) are made 'in the image of God', so that in some way they reflect his nature without being themselves divine.

In deciding between these two main possibilities, it is important to note that the same word 'form' occurs again in v. 7 where Jesus assumes the *form of a slave*, and that in the same verse he is described as *bearing the human likeness*. This strongly indicates that Jesus took on the human likeness at some later point after being in the form of God. It also suggests – most importantly – that the *form of God* is primarily to be associated with having the status of God, namely sovereignty, which was exchanged for the status of a slave.

All this shows, then, that we are to think of Jesus as sharing the status and function of God which is expressed in supreme sovereignty, and that it is the sheer contrast between supreme sovereignty and utter humiliation which is the point of the passage.

Despite this position of status, Jesus did not do what might have been expected of him. *He laid no claim to equality with God.* If we start with the phrase *equality with God*, this can suggest ideas of being on a level with God and therefore of having the same sovereign power as he has or of being able to act independently of him. These ideas are not very different from each other, and the thought of being equal with God might be thought to be included in being in the form of God.

But this brings us to what is probably the most difficult phrase in the passage, the phrase *laid no claim*. The original Greek of this is literally 'he did not regard equality with God as a *harpagmos*'.

This Greek word can be understood in two main ways.

(1) It can have an active sense and mean 'an act of seizing for one's own benefit', hence 'a means of self-aggrandizement'. On this view, Jesus did not regard his position of equality with God as a way of getting things for himself. He did not regard equality with God as consisting in snatching.

(2)   The word can also have a passive sense and mean 'something that is seized'. This gives rise to various possibilities:

(a)   He did not regard equality with God as something [not yet gained and] to be grasped after. (Cf. GNB: 'he did not think that by force he should try to become equal with God.') On this view, equality with God is something more than being in the form of God, and Jesus, who did not possess it, did not grasp after it. As the REB puts it, more mildly than GNB, *he laid no claim to equality with God.*

This possibility fits in nicely with the interpretation that the passage is about the human Jesus being in the form of God, like Adam and Eve. Paul could have been thinking of the story of Eve (and her husband), made in the image of God but who aspiring to 'be like God' when tempted by the serpent (Gen. 3.5, 22). However, in that story the likeness with God consists in 'knowing good and evil', which is somewhat different from the present passage which is concerned with sovereignty and power.

A major problem with this interpretation is whether *equality with God* is something different from being *in the form of God*. In our view this is unlikely, since, as we have noted, being in the form of God is defined by contrast with *assuming the form of a slave*.

(b)   He did not regard equality with God as something to be held on to or clutched greedily. He was willing to surrender it. This appears to be the interpretation adopted in the NIV: 'did not consider equality with God something to be grasped' (cf. JB: 'he did not cling to his equality with God').

(c)   He did not regard equality with God as something to be exploited. The idea here is that a person possesses something which can be utilized in a particular way. For example, a person might find something very valuable hidden away in an attic and decide to take advantage of it by selling it and using the money to have an expensive holiday. Or a person who has been promoted to a high rank in the army might use his position to exert his authority and impose upon other people so that they are forced to do what he wants. So the thought is of using what one has for one's own advantage.

This last possibility has been strongly defended in some recent discussions of the passage, and it has much to be said for it.

On the interpretation discussed above, the point of the statement is that Jesus could have used the position of equality with God which he already possessed as a means of self-aggrandizement, of furthering his own ends. It is possible, but not certain, that there is a contrast with Adam's different course of action.

2.7   This is the key verse in the passage, describing, as it does, what Christ actually did do in contrast to what he might have done (but did not do). But the meaning, especially of the first phrase, has been the object of much controversy. *He made himself nothing* is literally 'he emptied himself'.

Although the literal translation is not very meaningful, it is the best place from which to start in forming an interpretation.

(1) The phrase might mean that he emptied himself of something that he already had. One specific interpretation of this was that he gave up the divine attributes which he possessed – the power, knowledge and so on. This would give a biblical basis for the doctrine that in the incarnation Christ was divested of the powers of divinity, becoming ignorant instead of omniscient, weak instead of omnipotent, and local instead of omnipresent. This understanding of the effects of the incarnation is sometimes called 'kenoticism' (from the Greek verb *kenoo* used in this verse).

However, this view of the passage is not at all likely, since there is nothing in the context to suggest that Paul was thinking of these divine attributes, and indeed it could be argued that this way of thinking about God belongs to the theology of a later age.

It should be observed that the truth or otherwise of the 'kenotic' theory in theology is not entirely dependent upon our understanding of this passage. But since it has little to do with this verse we shall not consider it here.

(2) He gave up his existence in the form of God. But it is not clear how a person can give up or surrender the way in which he exists. Talk of 'being in the form of God' and talk of 'emptying oneself of something' belong to two different realms of discourse.

(3) He retained his position of equality with God, but made no use of it. This interpretation is again hard to get from the Greek.

(4) The REB 'he made himself nothing', if taken in the sense of 'he said No to his own desires' probably comes close to the meaning. The thought is that he gave up the exercise of sovereignty in order to become a servant. Instead of following whatever desires of his own he might have had and which he could sovereignly have carried through, he chose to say No to his own desires and No to the exercise of the powers which he could have used, and to do something else instead.

(5) As a development of this view we have the suggestion of N. T. Wright: he saw that 'self-negation [was] the proper expression of divine character', or, in other words, that the true use of equality with God lay in a vocation of humiliation and servanthood. This may be to press the point rather too hard. Yet in essence it is surely true. Here was a person who had (or could claim) equality with God and use that position of supreme power for his own ends but who chose not to do so but to serve God. Is this not to say that Jesus showed that the proper use of divine power was not in selfish action (like the gods of the Greeks) but in self-giving action?

The most probable interpretation is that Jesus refused to use his position of equality with God for selfish ends, but was prepared to say 'No' to himself. What this meant in fact is then expressed in terms of *assuming the form of a slave*. The words used deliberately echo what was said in v. 6 and emphasize the contrast between the form of God and that of a slave, between what Christ originally was and what he assumed. A slave is a person who obeys, who does what is commanded instead of giving commands. If we ask to whom Christ was obedient, the answer must be that he was obedient to God. The contrast is between being equal with God and obeying God.

The third phrase, *bearing the human likeness*, takes the thought a stage further. As in Romans 8.3 it means that he took on a human form. (The REB does not bring out sufficiently the fact that 'he became like man' (GNB).) The phrase does not mean that he became 'like' a man without actually becoming a real man, any more than *in the form of God* means that he was like God but did not actually share God's nature or status. Nor does the phrase necessarily imply that he gave up being like God in order to be like man. (In Rom. 8.3 it is God's own Son who appears in human form: he does not cease to be God's Son when he appears in human form.) There is no indication that Jesus was in any way other than truly human in the phrase. He was not like some of the gods in Greek mythology who could turn themselves into human form but still only appear <u>like</u> human beings.

2.8 The next phrase appears to gather up what has just been said before the thought is developed further. But the translation *sharing the human lot* does not bring out the full force of the phrase. Paul is not saying simply that Jesus shared the lot of human beings, but that 'he appeared in human likeness' (GNB). In appearance and in all other respects he appeared in the form of a man. There is probably an emphasis on the fact that this was how Jesus appeared to other people; instead of appearing as a lordly, divine figure, he was seen simply as a human being.

And it was while he was in this condition that *he humbled himself*. He had already done so by taking the form of a servant, but now he did so to the fullest extent, namely by being obedient, *even to the point of death*. The REB translation rightly makes it clear that he did not obey death itself, as if death was the master; rather, he was obedient to God (no other master is in view) even to the point of death. The idea that he entered the dominion of death is not present. More probably, we have a further allusion to the role of the Servant of Yahweh who humbled himself (Isa. 53.4, 8; cf. Acts 8.33), was obedient (Isa. 53.7) and poured himself out in death (Isa. 53.12).

As if that were not total humiliation for one who had been *in the form of God*, Paul adds that he died a *death on a cross*!. Plenty of contemporary evidence indicates that crucifixion was accounted not only the most diabolical of all forms of painful execution but also the most degrading and shameful, reserved as it was for criminals, slaves and non-Romans and subjecting the victim to intense humiliation as he hung helpless on the gibbet. In this way Paul brings out the stark reality of what 'humbling' oneself means – and thus provides a vivid commentary on how he understood 'humbly' in v. 3.

2.9   The passage has thus reached a climax in the humble death of Jesus, and from this point the mood changes. This change is marked most strikingly by the way in which there is a shift of subject. No longer are we told what Jesus did. Now God is the subject, and the theme is what he did in respect of Jesus.

As with the first part of the passage, the thought is expressed in a rhythmical prose with a certain amount of parallelism, and the pattern of thought is as follows:

> *Therefore God raised him to the heights*
> *and bestowed on him the name above all names,*
> > *that at the name of Jesus every knee should bow*
> > *– in heaven, on earth, and in the depths –*
> > *and every tongue acclaim, 'Jesus Christ is Lord,'*
> > *to the glory of God the Father.*

The introductory *therefore* indicates that what God did was in consequence of the self-humbling and obedience of Jesus. His reaction is expressed in two parallel clauses.

First, *God raised him to the heights*. This phrase is not very helpful to English readers because it is not a part of normal speech. The verb (literally 'to raise exceedingly high') was used metaphorically of assigning a person to a high status so that they received honour and praise, obedience and submission from other people of lower status (e.g. Ps. 97.9). The meaning here, then, is that God raised up Jesus from his position of humiliation and assigned him a high status. The following phrase shows that in fact Jesus is assigned the highest status possible; there is nobody else on the same level.

The question has been asked as to whether this new status was higher than that which he possessed at the outset when he was equal with God. But it is difficult to see how there could be a higher status than that. Therefore, it is more probable that the verb conveys the idea of a public manifestation of status. We may compare the way in which a king might bring his son, who as his son is already of princely status, before the people and give him a public investiture which recognizes that status and is the occasion for the people's acknowledgment of it. Thus there is a contrast between the public spectacle of Jesus 'sharing the human lot' in humble and even shameful circumstances and Jesus openly exalted.

But why should God do this? Why does this follow on as the consequence of the humiliation of Jesus? What is the logic of the opening *therefore*? Behind it may lie a spiritual law, 'whoever humbles himself shall be exalted' (Luke 14.11; 18.14), which God puts into operation. Or there may be an echo of the way in which God exalted his Servant (Isa. 52.13; cf. 53.12). But this doesn't explain why there is such a principle.

It is possible that the idea of a simple reward for humility is inadequate. Rather, by exalting Jesus God sets his stamp of approval on what Jesus did. God was vindicating the action of Jesus. He was openly declaring that the right thing for people to do is to forego their own rights and to be humbled.

There is, in other words, a danger that if the eternal reward for humiliation in this world is known to be future glory and high status, then people may voluntarily undergo humiliation, self-sacrifice and so on here in order to get a high status where it really matters, in the eternal kingdom of God. Such humiliation is a sham, since its motive is self-exaltation. What is seen in Jesus is self-humiliation in obedience to God and for the sake of other people.

So the point is not so much that Jesus is exalted as that by this action God sets his stamp of approval on self-humiliation and concern for the need of others. For elsewhere in Paul it is plainly taught that it was for our sakes that Jesus became poor (II Cor. 8.9), and in the writings of John the glory of Jesus is seen precisely in his dying on the cross. The thing that is praiseworthy is serving others, even to the point of death, and true glory is not the gaining of status but the performance of service.

In the second phrase the exaltation of Jesus is seen in that God *bestowed on him the name above all names*. A name is a significant word, and in the ancient world many names still retained their original force. Modern names by contrast tend to have degenerated into pure labels. Few people naming a child 'John' do so because they regard him as a 'gift of God' but in the Bible the corresponding Hebrew name retained this force. The name is thus an indicator of a characteristic of a person, and what God does is to give Jesus a name which is significant. This name is probably the title of Lord, and its significance is that it indicates a status superior to that of anybody else.

There is some uncertainty regarding the name which is bestowed. Two different answers have been proposed in the light of the following verses.

(1) Since it is *at the name of Jesus* that everybody will bow (v. 10) the name could simply be *Jesus* which is now invested with supreme status. The difficulty with this suggestion is that Jesus already bore this name right from his birth, whereas an action of naming after his death is surely indicated.

(2) In v. 11 we read how everybody will confess *Jesus Christ is Lord*. Now the name or title of *Lord* is the same as that of God himself, and it is noticeable that the gospel writers (with the exception of Luke) avoid using it of Jesus before his death. (When people address him as 'Lord', they are using a polite form of respectful address like our 'Sir' which could be used to anybody.) It is much more probable, therefore, that Paul's point is that God declared Jesus to be the Lord – in fact the Lord who is superior to all other beings. The point is that henceforth, when the name of 'Jesus' is uttered, it signifies a person who is the Lord.

2.10 The next verse fills out what has just been said. The point of giving Jesus a new name which brings supreme status is that when the simple name of Jesus is announced the result is that everybody present bows in worship and homage. One can think of modern situations where the announcement that a chairman or similar person is entering the room is a signal to everybody present to stand respectfully; at a wedding for instance the striking up of a traditional bridal march announces to everybody that the bride is now entering the church, and everybody stands in greeting and respect. So too Paul pictures people gathered together and when the name of 'Jesus' is called out and he walks in, everybody worships him. The audience is a universal one. It embraces the inhabitants of all three 'levels' of the universe. Whether we are to think literally of three levels is uncertain; Paul was obviously writing in terms of the spatial geography of his day which comprehended all reality in terms of this world and what lies above and below it, all three levels being regarded as inhabited by different beings, human and superhuman.

The language used of Jesus here is very significant because it is an echo of words in Isa. 45.23 which are used of the acclamation given to God himself. The honour traditionally reserved for God is given also to Jesus.

2.11 The immediately following words which tell us that *every tongue* will *acclaim* him are drawn from the same passage. In full it reads:

> From every corner of the earth
> turn to me and be saved;
> for I am God, there is none other.
> By my life I have sworn,
> I have given a promise of victory,
> a promise that will not be broken;
> to me every knee will bow,
> by me every tongue will swear,
> saying, 'In the Lord alone
> are victory and might.' (Isa. 45.22f.)

What is interesting here is the fact that this passage, which is applied by Paul elsewhere to God the Father (Rom. 14.11), so strongly emphasizes that there is only one God, and yet here Paul applies these words to Jesus rather than to God. Nothing could convey more clearly how in the eyes of Paul the one who had plumbed the lowest depths in humble service is now given a position than which nothing higher is conceivable.

It is, however, important to observe that the final comment is *to the glory of God the Father*. Paul avoids any tendency that there might have been to replace God by Christ or to suggest that Christ was superior to God or that it was matter of indifference whether people worshipped God or Christ. The bottom line is that the paying of respect to Jesus is a way of honouring God. It has to be so, because the position held by Jesus was assigned to him by God; honouring God involves honouring those whom he has placed in a position of honour, and since honouring them is an honouring of persons whose rank has been assigned by God it is implicitly an honouring of God himself.

Paul's language has been thought to indicate that a time is coming when all created beings will honour Jesus Christ as Lord. Since honouring Jesus Christ as Lord was the mark of the Christian believer, it can then be urged that Paul looks forward to all created beings accepting him as Saviour. This, however, is undoubtedly a mistaken interpretation of what Paul is saying here. His concern is to underline the position of Jesus and therefore his point is that, if anybody is to be universally honoured, it is he; if people are going to give supreme honour to anybody, Jesus is the one whom they ought to honour. It does not follow that everybody will necessarily do so. Yet it is also the case that in Romans 14.11 we have the statement that everybody will give account of himself to God, and therefore it may be better to take this passage to mean simply that when it comes to the day of judgment all creatures will be subject to Jesus as they are to God. It again does not follow that all will grasp at salvation; by that point it will be too late to do so.

THE SIGNIFICANCE OF THE 'HYMN'

What is the point of the passage as a whole?

First, it is impossible to avoid the conclusion that Jesus is here presented as an example to be followed. His example of service to God is clearly a pattern for Christians to emulate in their mutual relationships. They are, of course, to serve God, as the application in v. 12 will make clear. But the starting point which led to the use of the example of Jesus was the need to think of the needs and interests of others.

Second, the readers must inevitably have been led to ask why it was that Jesus followed this particular path. It has often been said that this passage says nothing about the cross as a means of salvation (and this has been a reason for denying that Paul composed it), but it is doubtful whether this element can be entirely eliminated from the passage. The parallel with II Cor. 8.9, where the one who was rich became poor that we through his poverty might become rich, spells out a thought which, while not explicit here, must have been aroused in the minds of those who read these words. To speak of the cross was to speak of the means of salvation: Paul could not use the word without this thought being suggested. Further the words *Jesus Christ is Lord* constituted the confession made by Christians when they entered on the Christian way and experienced the power of the Spirit in their lives. The thought of Christ as Saviour is thus sufficiently indicated in the passage at point after point. (And if Christian ears were tuned to picking up OT allusions in their context, then Isa. 45.21f. would also raise thoughts of salvation.)

Thirdly the acclamation of Jesus as Lord, using the very words that formed part of the early Christian confession, reminds the readers implicitly that they accept Jesus as Lord – and therefore are committed to the way of life which he exemplified. They are part of the company who must confess Jesus Christ as Lord. They must obey God as he did, and such obedience will include acceptance of the instructions which God's apostle gives to them regarding their communal behaviour.

To become a Christian, then, was to acknowledge Jesus as Lord, and in the light of the present verse, that confession came to include the belief that Jesus shared the status of God and was entitled to the same name of 'Lord' that was borne in the Scriptures by God himself.

The outworking of salvation in the life of the church
2.12–18

The final part of this section draws the practical conclusion from the description of Jesus Christ. The essential point is made in v. 14. This is preceded by a general statement about the need for obedience to God expressed in terms of working out salvation (vv. 12–13), and it is followed by another statement which expresses what will be the practical consequences of unity in the church community (vv.

15–18). One consequence is the effect on the surrounding non-Christian community. The other is the way in which Paul's work will be brought to completion and not undone by the failure of the church. The path envisaged for them will not be easy, any more than it was for Paul, but it will in fact be a joyful one if they are prepared to take it.

2.12 Paul marks the end of the descriptive passage and the beginning of a fresh appeal to his readers by the device of addressing them as *my friends* (cf. 3.1; 4.1, 8). His line of argument, expressed by *so you too* is clearly: just as Jesus your Lord was obedient, so you must be obedient in working out your salvation. But he wants to encourage the readers and also to show that he is not asking something fresh from them but merely reinforcing what he has said previously. And so he says that they must go on working *as* they have *always* done. Further, he is aware of the psychological consideration that 'when the cat's away the mice will play'; his readers are prone to this weakness, like anybody else, and therefore he urges them to be active when he is absent from them and not able to see what they are doing. Indeed, it is all the more creditable if they can endeavour to be *even more* active in his absence than in his presence.

OBEDIENCE IN THE CHURCH

Paul is no doubt thinking here primarily of obedience to God (as was shown by Jesus, 2.8), but equally he saw himself as the channel (or one of the channels) by which God's instructions came to them.

Some writers have accused Paul of manipulating his congregations, forcing them into obedience to himself by such devices as presenting his instructions to them with the indication that they are really God's commands. It is doubtful whether the accusation can be made to stick. Two points are worth making.

The first is that, if people are to know God's instructions for them as individuals and as a group, then inevitably some means of communication must be employed. The exposition of biblical teaching is one such means. The task of the preacher or Bible teacher is thus one of immense responsibility in acting as the interpreter of God's will.

The second point is that teachers have to be extraordinarily careful that what is taught is God's will and not their own personal fancies. It is fatally easy to deceive ourselves on this point, and therefore considerable restraint is needed.

The specific instruction to the readers is: *work out your own salvation*.

This curious expression has been understood in three main ways:

1. The readers are to work at the spiritual health of the church as a group. This interpretation fits in nicely with the need for developing a spirit of unity and love in their mutual relationships. The difficulty is that this is a most unusual use of the word 'salvation'.

2. The readers are to work at their own individual salvation, in the sense that they are to express its consequences in their lives. Here we see the word 'salvation' being used to refer to the sum of the spiritual gifts which people receive in this life.

3. The readers are to work towards their own salvation, with salvation being understood as the future goal of their endeavours. This would tie in with the way in which Paul often refers to salvation or to being saved as the state into which believers enter at the last judgment and the parousia (cf. 3.20 where Jesus comes as Saviour at his parousia).

We should probably accept the view that the readers are to work at expressing the consequences of their own salvation (view 2. above). It is supported by the fact that in the next verse Paul speaks about what God is already doing *in* the readers, and then in the following verses he is concerned with the outward manifestation of their Christian lives.

In fear and trembling is a strange phrase to accompany this command. Similar language is used in the OT of the terror that struck people faced by divine activity (Ex. 15.16; Deut. 2.25; 9.19; 11.25; Ps. 54.5; Isa. 19.16; (cf. I Cor. 2.3; II Cor. 7.15; Eph. 6.5; Heb. 12.21) cf. Judith 2.28; IV Macc. 4.10). The phrase is placed very emphatically in the Greek text and the language is strong, but the emphasis arises from the consideration in the next verse that God is at work in the congregation. It contrasts with the casual way in which people may take their Christian faith, ignoring the sovereignty of God and treating him as if he didn't matter.

2.13   *It is God who works in you* conveys the idea of a divine influence of a powerful character which energizes the readers. It is a kind of spiritual impetus, comparable perhaps to the way in which a person may feel full of zest for action after taking some kind of stimulant.

Paul – and the NT writers generally – evidently believed that there was some way in which a spiritual power could exercise an influence on the human will, mind and emotions. There is no easy analogy to this. We may think how a dominant personality may sway other people, making them feel capable and zealous to do things of which they would not otherwise feel able, but something more than that is meant.

In this case the effect of the divine influence is twofold; it inspires *both the will and the deed*. It produces encouragement to do certain things and then the ability to actually carry them out. What is done is *for his own chosen purpose*. This is the best translation of a phrase which expresses the intention that God inspires believers to have, namely to do what will forward God's purpose.

The Work of God and the Work of the Believer

These two verses together express in sharp form the paradox of Christian existence. Paul can tell his readers that God is working in them so that they want to do and will do what is according to his purpose, yet at the same time he urges them (both here and repeatedly elsewhere) to do God's will and recognizes that, left to themselves, people will often fail to do it, whether through ignorance or through weakness or through the force of temptations. There is no easy way of reconciling these two factors. Both are true of our experience at different times. Sometimes we feel particularly conscious of a power greater than our own that enables us to do what we otherwise could not do. At other times we are conscious of our failure to do as we should. Both are parts of normal Christian experience. Equally, it is not possible to 'let go and let God' as a popular slogan puts it, to hand over our lives to God and expect that his power will work automatically in our lives. Moral and spiritual effort is continually required.

The point is an important one. On the one hand, there are preachers who hold that it is possible to be 'instantaneously sanctified' just as one can be instantaneously 'born again'. If we accept the Spirit of God into our lives, victory over temptation should be a real and complete possibility. On the other hand, we have the suggestion that the Christian religion is a matter of moral effort by our own power, and the most that we are given is a clean sheet, a pattern to follow, and encouragement to persevere. Paul's teaching supports neither extreme, but in a way that resists definition claims both that the power of God is at work in us and that we have to put effort into Christian living; that is surely confirmed by our experience as Christians. There are occasions when we know that we could not have resisted temptation or seized an opportunity to do good apart from some power higher than ourselves; and there are others when we know that we have had to summon all our resources of will to do what we ought to do.

2.14   The general principle is now applied to the specific problem that faced the church. Working out their own salvation means quite concretely: *Do everything without grumbling or argument*. It is assumed that grumbling and arguing are wrong for Christians (cf. I Cor. 10.10). It is sufficient, therefore, to issue a command against them. And it is one that the readers should be able to fulfil.

2.15   Although the REB suggests that this verse contains a set of further commands to be placed alongside those in the previous verse, in fact the structure of the Greek sentence shows that it really gives the purpose of the preceding commands. The readers are exhorted not to grumble and argue in order that they may be *innocent and above reproach*. What Paul is saying is that the absence of these undesirable qualities will give the readers a particular reputation in the surrounding world. People will see how they live and comment: 'They say that they are followers of Jesus, and they do hold some strange ideas that are not suitable for Romans, but you can't deny that their conduct is blameless; why, they don't even quarrel with one another!' And some people might go further and probe more positively into this strange religion that produced followers with lives of such a quality.

But Paul may have something else in mind. When he says that the readers are to be *faultless children of God in a crooked and depraved generation*, his words echo Deut. 32.5 where the Israelites are described as people 'who sinned; they were not his children, blameworthy, a crooked and depraved generation'. Paul contrasts the sinful, faithless and grumbling ways of the Israelites going through the desert from Egypt to Canaan with the ideal attitude of Christians. Where the Israelites failed, the followers of Jesus are meant to succeed! Whether Paul intended any kind of contrast with the Jews of his own day who had rejected Jesus as the Messiah it is hard to say. We shall meet people who could have answered to this description in ch. 3, and we have already come across the people in Paul's place of imprisonment who were motivated by self-interest in preaching the gospel. The thought of either of these groups may have influenced Paul at this point.

The effect of this blameless way of life is summed up in the thought that the readers will *shine like stars in a dark world*. This expression may simply mean that they appear as bright spots in an otherwise dark picture, or it may imply that they bring light to the world around them. In the latter case we have the thought of a Christian witness which brings light to others. So the question is whether the readers act as Christian witnesses bringing light that helps other people or whether the light is merely a sign of their own salvation and illumination . The word 'light' is used of the heavenly bodies which shed light on the world. And the language of Dan. 12.3 does speak of those who lead others to righteousness. It seems likely, therefore, that Paul is thinking of the way in which the good lives of Christians are a form of witness to the world around them.

2.16   The thought continues with the statement that such people *proffer the word of life*. The thought is of offering something to other people. It continues the idea of evangelism.

> The Greek verb might mean simply 'to hold fast' (for one's own good, with no thought of helping other people). The line of thought could then be simply that Paul will be able to exult in the readers themselves on the day of judgment, provided that they are blameless, shine on account of their good deeds, and hold fast to the truth without giving it up. But the verb can certainly mean 'offer, hold out', and the thought of being evangelistically effective fits into the context without difficulty.

But Paul puts the concept into the context of his own task as a missionary. He wants – on a human level – to be able to display the fruits of his work at the day of assessment. He works with a view to what will happen on the day of Christ. He does not want to feel that he ran or laboured in vain. Both expressions – *to run* and to *labour* – are Pauline phrases for missionary work. It is interesting that the same language is used of the Servant of Yahweh in Isa. 49.4, but it was perhaps a common turn of phrase, and we cannot say for certain that this is a deliberate allusion. *The day of Christ* is the day of judgment, which in the eyes of Paul involves an assessment of what Christians have done with their lives as well as a separation of the righteous from the unrighteous.

SEEING THINGS FROM A LONG-TERM PERSPECTIVE

Paul's thought here is couched in terms of an ultimate verdict on his work. He is concerned about what is of value when measured in terms of eternity. A person may win short-term benefits or enjoy temporary pleasures, and for many people life consists simply in enjoying the pleasures of the present moment rather than in working towards some more permanent end. A person may, for example, spend their wages recklessly on whatever momentarily takes their fancy; another may save up to buy something that will give longer term pleasure; yet another may have a still longer vision. Paul's way of thinking shows that he looked to the ultimate values of life, and saw these as being measured by the day of judgment.

2.17   It was possible that Paul's work as a missionary could prove to be fatal. He could pour out his *life-blood* like a form of ancient sacrifice known as a drink-offering (e.g. Num. 15.8–10). When an animal was being sacrificed on an altar, a liquid (usually wine or oil) might be poured out on top of it as a sort of secondary offering. Here Paul thinks of himself as being poured out in this way, the major sacrifice being that of the Philippians themselves. The same phrase is used of Paul dying for the sake of Christ in II Tim. 4.6, and this may suggest that here too he has in mind the possibility that his work for Christ may involve his own death – whether through physical exhaustion or through martyrdom.

It is not clear whether the present tense that Paul uses here indicates a process that is already happening or a future possibility. The force of 'even if' might suggest that he is contemplating something that is possibility rather than actuality, but it is perhaps more likely that he is thinking of his present imprisonment as part of his self-offering for the sake of the gospel. The Greek verb translated *my life-blood is to be poured out* is literally 'I am offered' and need not refer only to death.

The Philippians themselves are engaged in what is here described as *the sacrifice and offering up of* their *faith*. There is no indication that their death is in mind here. The sacrifice arises out of their faith or consists of their faith. So too does the service. The sacrifice and service must be offered to God. The whole of their Christian life must be contained in the expression.

The experience must have been a painful or harsh one for Paul. Otherwise, there is no point in saying '[even] if', which implies a contrast with the rejoicing that follows. But why does he say that he rejoices? Surely because in their sacrificial activity he sees the proof of the reality of their faith and can rejoice in it. But he also rejoices with them. This suggests that he rejoices in his own sufferings just as they [should] do in theirs, and he shares in their rejoicing. Similarly, if they do rejoice in their own suffering, they will be able also to rejoice with him in his sufferings. In the same way he tells the Ephesians not to be disheartened by his tribulations for their sakes, which are their glory (Eph 3.13). They are to rejoice at what is happening in his life and share in his joy. All this may suggest that the church itself was disheartened by its experiences and needed the special emphasis on joy that is characteristic of this letter (see on 1.4).

THE LIFE OF THE CHURCH

This section brings to a conclusion the main section of the letter discussing the need for unity, love and humility in the church. Paul is concerned with unity within the local church, and may have in mind disputes between different smaller groups (e.g. house fellowships) within it. The crucial point is that the individual believer's experience of salvation must find expression in the communal life of the group. Paul clearly expects groups of believers to show a quality of life which is not matched in the surrounding world; he obviously believes that Christians have a moral ideal and the ability to reach it which is not found elsewhere. He is probably also saying that Christians must display this way of life in order to bring light to the world and persuade it to heed the gospel. He does not hold back from suggesting that the spiritual growth of the church affects his own personal position at the judgment. And he recognizes that the Christian life is going to involve suffering, discomfort and hardship of various sorts – even the pain of harsh persecution; even as he faces these things, he can encourage his readers to share his own feelings of joy which spring from his experience of salvation.

None of this requires any translation to fit the needs of the church today. It just requires some plain speaking! One added dimension today, however, is the need for unity and love between different congregations and branches of the church.

Future visits to Philippi by Paul and his colleagues
2.19–30

A new major section now begins in which Paul is basically concerned to give news regarding the forthcoming visits of Timothy and Epaphroditus to the church. The visit of Timothy would obviously be subsequent to the letter and hopefully precede Paul's own visit to the church. The visit, or rather return, by Epaphroditus is probably to be associated with the sending of the letter (otherwise we would have to postulate yet another messenger being sent to the church, but Paul says that he has nobody other than Timothy whom he considers it appropriate to send). In both cases Paul gives a kind of commendation of the visitor.

The importance of personal contacts between Christians stands out clearly in this section. Persons working for Christ away from home (or separated from their families and friends for other reasons) can become lonely and dispirited, and the feelings expressed here are very natural. In such circumstances it was right and proper for Paul to do what he could to arrange for meetings and trips that brought people together.

There is nothing sinister on Paul's side in what he says. Natural loving concern is all that is indicated. But the possibility of people serving the Lord out of selfish interest and not truly caring for the Lord is mentioned, and we may plausibly link this reference with that in ch. 1 to people who preached the gospel from wrong motives.

This should not surprise us. The church consists of people who live in community and love, and therefore the promotion of personal links and loving relationships is an essential part of its activity. They may be on a very human level, but again this is not surprising, because the church should represent the perfecting of human relationships.

Timothy's planned visit to Philippi
2.19–24

The purpose of Timothy's visit was primarily so that he could come back and bring news to Paul about the church. And the choice of him for the task was because he had a good record as a worker alongside Paul and had a concern for the Philippians that was not shared by anybody else who was with Paul. (This comment may perhaps refer only to people who might be free to undertake such a journey.)

The uncertainty regarding the timing of the visit may be connected with the fact that Paul needed him with himself, especially if he had nobody else like-minded to assist him in his present situation.

2.19   When Paul writes of his *hope in the Lord Jesus*, he means that the basis of his hope lies in the fact that Christ has a good purpose for his church and will act to make it possible. Hope is not a vague longing that certain good things will take place in the future which has no real basis; it is rather a statement of confidence, and the confidence has a solid foundation, in this case the power and the goodness of Christ which has already been experienced and proved in various ways. Hope is thus the extension of faith into the future. It is faith that the Lord will act in certain ways.

Timothy was an appropriate choice for the visit to Philippi because he was already known to the church. According to Acts 16 he had accompanied Paul from Lystra on his mission that took him across to Macedonia. *Soon* is of course 'soon after the letter arrives'. Paul did not know of anybody else who would be visiting Philippi or travelling from there to him before Timothy, and therefore an important part of Timothy's visit would be his return to Paul with news about the church – which Paul assumes will be good news. There is therefore a note of encouragement and confidence here which the church would overhear. Implicit in the statement is Paul's hope that they for their part would be cheered by the good news that they would be getting about himself, no doubt primarily through this letter rather than only through Timothy.

2.20   Timothy is warmly commended to the church. The force of the statement may be primarily to commend him as the person with the highest concern for the church, but it is impossible to avoid the negative implications – there were other people not so concerned for the church.

2.21   These other people were concerned with self-interest. They sought their own interests, not those of Christ. Presumably they are related to the contentious people mentioned in 1.15–17. The language is strong, perhaps hyperbolic. It echoes what Paul said in 2.4 where he mentioned people looking after their own interests and not those of other people (cf. I Cor. 10.24, 33; 13.5) Thus here we have something that was also a problem in Philippi itself, and it may well be, therefore, that an incidental purpose of Paul in this passage is to present negative and positive examples from which the church could learn.

2.22   Timothy's worth was known to the church – confirmation that he had been there with Paul and they had had a chance to see him for themselves. He had worked like a slave for the gospel in company with Paul just as a son would serve his father in obedience (2.12!). Paul regularly thinks of Timothy as a child despite his adult status; he is somewhat conscious of a gap between himself and the younger man, which was probably more marked in the ancient world than it would be today. It may well be too that Timothy was somewhat diffident in manner, and that some of the churches did not have a high regard for his capabilities; nevertheless, for Paul his spiritual qualities more than made up for any absence of natural gifts.

2.23   Paul's intention to send Timothy, therefore, is appropriate. The only uncertainty concerned the time when he would come, and that depended on the development of Paul's own situation about which we know so little that we cannot say precisely what would affect the time of Timothy's departure.

2.24   However, Timothy's trip was but a preliminary to Paul's own coming. It was a matter of uncertainty in that humanly speaking Paul did not know how or when it would be possible, but he had confidence that God would make it possible for him. That is to say, although he could not see how it would happen, he was confident that the Lord would open up the possibility – and if it did not prove possible, Paul would conclude that the Lord had other plans for him.

HUMAN PLANS AND GOD'S WILL

We thus see how in Paul's work there was a combination of what one might call human strategic planning and trusting in the Lord's planning. Paul could make plans about sending a representative to Philippi, and justify them on what we might call commonsense grounds: (a) that it was necessary to send somebody; (b) that Timothy was the right person; and (c) that he should be sent at a specific time. The timing, however, was dependent on things that were not in Paul's control. Paul, therefore, could do no more than trust that God would act in the situation to make possible both Timothy's and his own visits. The practical problem in the Christian life is to reach this balance between making human decisions and recognizing the purpose of God. There is no simple answer to it, and there cannot be. What is clear is that human planning must always be under the rubric 'if the Lord wills', and that God expects people to use their common sense.

Epaphroditus' return to Philippi
2.25–30

The return of Epaphroditus to Philippi appears to represent a change of plans. He was originally intended to stay with Paul. But he had been seriously ill and homesick, and the Philippians were naturally worried about him. It was therefore to their mutual advantage that he should return home, and he should receive a hero's welcome because of the suffering he had undergone to complete his work.

Reading between the lines we may suspect that Epaphroditus had some critics at home, who would think poorly of him if he did not stay longer with Paul and work harder. One suggestion is that possibly the Philippians were expecting Timothy or another of his colleagues to come to them from Paul, and that the arrival of Epaphroditus in his place would have been something of an unwelcome surprise; ought not Epaphroditus, illness or no illness, to have stayed with Paul in order to complete his assignment on their behalf? There could, therefore, have been some criticism of Epaphroditus when he arrived and even some disappointment at seeing him. That is why Paul has to defend him at some length and declare his confidence in him. Epaphroditus had not failed in his duty, and should be welcomed and honoured. His illness naturally made it sensible for him to return home to his friends (and family) rather than to stay on. We simply do not know sufficient about his illness and circumstances to judge the situation and certainly not to utter any criticism of him, as if he should have stuck it out and not returned home until later.

2.25 When Paul says that he had *decided* to send Epaphroditus home, the translation conceals the idea that Paul had come to the conclusion that it was necessary to do so because of the circumstances given in v. 26, namely that Epaphroditus was filled with longing for his friends and worried about their feelings. Taking this comment at its face value, (a) Epaphroditus was homesick, and Paul thought that in the circumstances it was best for him to return home; (b) Epaphroditus knew that his friends were worried about him, and that the best antidote to their worries was to actually see him alive and well. This reflects entirely natural human feelings. If somebody is seriously ill away from home, the relatives are not really happy until they have seen for themselves that the person is fully recovered – and in the absence of telephones and photographs and the like the actual return of the person is needed. If there was any criticism by some members of the church, Paul's answer was that Epaphroditus had in fact fully accomplished the task for which he had been sent (v. 30), even if he might have been able to do more in other circumstances.

Epaphroditus is described as being Paul's colleague. The term *brother* in this context suggests that Paul saw Epaphroditus as a fellow-missionary. *Fellow-worker* confirms this, and *comrade* is a military term indicating that they are fellow-soldiers in the same conflict (cf. 1.30). These words show that Paul fully accepted Epaphroditus as a sharer in the work of the gospel and saw nothing essential missing from his work. They are an expression of confidence in him, but they also convey something of the nature of the task in which they were engaged, akin to a military campaign in its strenuousness and need for close cooperation.

At the same time Epaphroditus is also described in terms of his relation to the home church. He was *commissioned to attend to Paul's needs*. This translation conceals the way in which Epaphroditus is actually called their 'apostle' to Paul. The idea of the churches sending out workers with this designation is found in II Cor. 8.23. Just as there were apostles whose commission appears to have come direct from Jesus Christ, like Paul himself, so there were also persons authorized by individual congregations to share in the work of the Christian mission. Epaphroditus' particular task was to *attend to* the needs of Paul. The related word has already been used in 2.17 (where it is translated 'offering up'), and we saw that it refers to a service that is costly and munificent. Epaphroditus was thus sent to help specifically with the personal needs of Paul as a missionary; he was certainly the bearer of a gift in money or kind to help Paul in the privations of prison, and this is probably quite specifically in mind here. But the extent of his help surely went beyond that. We just do not know enough of Paul's situation to know how much he needed help from others and what kind of help he would require. The implication is that Epaphroditus did what was needed of him.

2.26 But the period of assistance to Paul ran into problems. Epaphroditus was longing to see the people at home – and communication by the slowness of the ancient postal system was no substitute. It is no good saying that Christ had called him to be a missionary and to practise self-denial and repress his natural feelings. He needed his friends and was distressed that they were worried about him. Again, this is something that is natural and understandable on the human level. Some people may not be worried in this kind of way – some are tougher-skinned than others – but there are people who are sensitive, and it is no use simply telling them to buck up and not to be so worried.

2.27 The fact was that Epaphroditus had been seriously ill, and if the story had reached home, it would undoubtedly have caused worry, especially because people could not see for themselves just how ill he was. If he was, as Paul says, at death's door, the concern would be all the greater – and exaggerated rumours could easily have arisen. The unmistakable implication is that he could well have died but for what Paul calls the mercy of God. Whether or not people die when they are seriously ill was, and is, not entirely in the hands of the doctors; there were less guarantees then than now that medical care would be successful – and there are still of course factors beyond medical control. So when Epaphroditus recovered, Paul could attribute it only to the mercy of God. (Had he been cured by the doctors, Paul would still have said the same thing. There is no 'God of the gaps' mentality here, only the recognition that the whole of life is in the hands of God.)

This was an act of divine mercy to Epaphroditus himself – who was spared dying away from his friends – but also to Paul who was spared bereavement. Thereby Paul was spared *one sorrow on top of another*, by which he means simply yet another sorrow on top of other disappointments. (One cannot be more specific, but it hasn't stopped commentators trying!)

2.28   Therefore Paul was *all the more eager* to send him – but this surely means rather 'with all the more urgency', ahead of the time originally planned. The situation had led to accelerated action for the good of the friends of Epaphroditus. Thereby one cause of Paul's sorrow would be removed, that due to his concern for the people at Philippi who were fretting over Epaphroditus.

2.29   But if Paul was taking this step, it was vital that the Philippians did their part by giving Epaphroditus a most loving welcome. They were to welcome him with honour and respect, such as was to be given to church leaders, and indeed they were to treat any people like Epaphroditus in the same kind of way. This may suggest that some people at Philippi may have been not altogether kindly disposed towards him.

2.30   The reason for the respect is finally summed up in the reminder that it was because of the work of Christ that he had nearly died. A direct line could be traced between his service for Christ and his almost fatal illness. In a real sense, therefore, the illness was part of the sufferings involved in apostolic work and witness. At the same time, it is clear that Epaphroditus himself had not shrunk from his task. If anybody might criticize him for lack of emotional stamina to continue with Paul and stay away from home, they could not do so with regard to the way in which he had in effect gambled with death. He had taken risks with his health to fulfil his task – like a person with a dangerous heart condition who exerts special effort to help somebody. In this way he had fully achieved what he set out to do, to complete the task laid on him by the church at Philippi.

Epaphroditus

Congregations appreciate stories rather than doctrine, and therefore it is useful when the doctrine can be conveyed as part of a story. Some NT characters are so colourless, or there is so little information about them, that they cannot be made the subjects of biographical sketches. (Beware of starting a series on the Twelve Disciples; there's not much that can be said about some of them beyond the importance of obscure servants of the Lord!) But (as in the case of Timothy) we know enough of Epaphroditus to make him a good subject. He stands out as an example of a human being with his weaknesses and his strengths which are tried and tested in the work of the church. It is important to stress Paul's human sympathy for him, which recognized his emotional needs and did something about them. The preacher will find in this section of the letter character studies which reveal people as they really are and do not idealize them in a false manner. They will note that there are qualities which are commended and which can be cultivated. They will observe the need for Christians to support and help one another.

And they will see how human emotions cannot be separated from the work of the gospel. God's workers are people with personal gifts and personal problems, and they are not simply unfeeling machines or instruments, resources to be used. Perhaps it is in the church that we are, or should be, most conscious of the links between people as people and their work. In the place of secular work, colleagues may never know about a person's personal life – their marriage, family, problems with a mortgage, hobbies, holidays, dependent relatives and so on – and these things may be (for the most part) irrelevant to the work being done. But life cannot be completely compartmentalized like that, and the work of the church – like social work and similar concerns – is closely tied to individual people and their personal lives.

Warning against Judaizers
3.1–4.1

This chapter takes up a new theme which has not been mentioned explicitly earlier in the letter. This in itself should not really constitute a problem, because a letter-writer may well have a number of different topics to discuss, just as Paul certainly has in some of his other letters. The dificulty is rather that the new topic is introduced abruptly and does not seem connected with the previous material.

As was indicated in the Introduction, the problem was the possible menace of rival missionaries who were following Paul around and arguing that his presentation of the gospel was wrong or defective. It was necessary for his Gentile converts to be circumcised and keep the other commandments of the Jewish law if they were to be truly saved and belong to the people of God. Paul's response was that the one thing that mattered was to be joined to Christ, and he cited his own example as one who had deliberately chosen to regard all his Jewish privileges as worthless (3.1–11).

It may well be that the missionaries claimed that Paul's teaching was just the 'first stage' for Gentile converts. To achieve what they called 'maturity' it was necessary to go further. Paul resisted the idea that anybody, himself included, was already all that they should be, and rather urged them all to follow the path to which Christ called them (3.12–16).

In even stronger language he finally warned against people whom he considered to be enemies of the cross by reason of their attitude to worldly things, and encouraged his converts with the thought that their present humble situation would be changed to glory at the coming of Christ (3.17–21).

THE JUDAIZERS AND THE PREACHER TODAY

This section of the letter raises difficulties for the preacher because it deals with a problem that is no longer present in this precise form. Judaizing is not one of the temptations threatening the average congregation today! How, then, can the preacher use a passage which deals with an anachronistic theme? Two lines of approach are promising.

On the one hand, preachers can readily take up the positive teaching of Paul about the place of Jesus Christ and develop this timeless message. See below for more on this approach.

On the other hand, they can enquire into the rationale and motives behind the Judaizing teaching and see whether these manifest themselves in other ways in the world today. The Judaizing movement has been understood in different ways.

Traditionally, it has been argued that the Judaizers were trying to put themselves in the right with God on the basis of keeping the law, and so acquiring some kind of 'merit' in his sight, of which they might be proud as being their own achievement. Alternatively, it has been pointed out that the Jews regarded themselves as being God's covenant people on the basis of his grace, and therefore they did not have to do anything to merit entry. The works of the law which they carried out had then to be regarded either as actions which they did in order to maintain their status as God's people or as badges which they wore to indicate that they did belong to the people of God.

On the former view, what Paul is attacking is reliance on human achievements as the basis of salvation. It can then be observed that elsewhere in some of the later NT writings the principle is broadened out. Reliance on human works of any kind is not the way to salvation: it depends entirely on divine grace (cf. Titus 3.5). It follows that any kind of dependence on human works is disqualified. The Reformers therefore rightly attacked the mediaeval Roman Catholic idea of a 'treasury of merits' – the idea that one could balance one's good deeds over against one's sins to secure justification – and the practice of indulgences, to insist that salvation was solely by grace through faith – and modern Catholicism would generally go along with this. But reliance on human merit to secure God's favour is endemic in humanity, and so the point can be extended to counter all kinds of merit-based religion.

It would also be right to attack any kind of teaching which insists that certain beliefs or practices are essential additions to faith in Christ. Sometimes adherence to a particular culture or life-style has become synonymous with the gospel. Converts have been persuaded to abandon their own culture and adopt a western life-style. Or within the church adherence to particular rules – e.g. a non-smoking rule – or ecclesiastical practices – e.g. believers's baptism – can be made to seem to be part of the faith-package. The problem sometimes is that a good case can be made for regarding some types of life-style as sinful and therefore inconsistent with faith in Christ or for seeing some practices as theologically necessary, and care is needed to distinguish the essential from our human traditions.

However, although the chapter does offer plenty of scope for attack on such things, the preacher should surely want to concentrate on the positive side. If Christ is truly the goal of the believer, then the other things will be seen in their proper persective.

Two sources of confidence
3.1–11

3.1 This verse is far from easy, and contains a number of problems. Despite the introductory *And*, the first part: *And now, my friends, I wish you joy in the Lord*, has no direct connection with what precedes. Nor does the sentence seem to be connected with what follows. A further problem lies in how to translate the verb. REB interprets the imperative form '[you] rejoice' as a wish by Paul – *I wish you joy*. It is doubtful whether this is a correct interpretation, and probably we should revert to the traditional rendering.

The word 'And' is not there in the Greek. Although REB prints the sentence as the conclusion to the paragraph just ending, this is unlikely to be correct. It is better to see 'now' as the introduction to a new section and topic, as in 4.8. Although the NRSV mg translation of the verb as 'Farewell' is a possible rendering, it wrongly assumes that this verse is part of the ending of the letter.

We find similar problems in 4.4 where the same words occur, and where again they seem to form a command on their own. An explanation must be found which will account for both verses.

We propose that the verse looks forwards. The stress lies on *in the Lord*, and the command 'rejoice' has its roots in the situation and perhaps in the thinking of the Philippians. The letter contains several references to being confident or exulting in the Lord or in Christ. Paul's point could therefore be that Christians have a basis for joy and confidence in the Lord – and not anywhere else. Thus what Paul advocates in this verse stands as a superscription to what is to follow. The source of the Christian's joy and confidence is the Lord – and not any human achievements, qualifications or practices. This is then developed negatively over against the Judaizers.

This explanation will also hold for 4.4, where the readers are encouraged to rejoice in the Lord despite the pressures on them from outside. Paul is developing a line of thought found earlier in 2.18 where he encourages the readers to rejoice despite the fear of external pressure on them and despite the tendency to grumble and be miserable.

Paul says that he does not find it burdensome to repeat what he has written before – and indeed it is for the good of the readers. This could mean that what he has just said about rejoicing in the Lord is a repetition of what he had said or written (2.18!) earlier.

REB assumes that Paul is repeating what he has *written* before, but it is also possible that he is referring to what he had said previously when he was with them (cf. 3.18). If v. 1a is the introduction to what Paul is about to say about putting one's trust and confidence in the Lord (and not in the rites of Judaism or anything else), then it is possible that he is referring back to earlier occasions when he had spoken about this particular danger.

3.2   We now move into a warning against people whose teaching Paul considered to be dangerous for the church. The general tone suggests that they were people from outside the church with a message that differed in significant respects from Paul's. The church is thus told to watch out for them, in the sense of recognizing such people if and when they appear, and not being taken in by their message. It may be that these people had not yet visited Philippi, but they were known to be active and so advance warning was given.

They are described, first, as *those dogs*. This is obviously a rude and derogatory expression; it is quite strong language. Jews were known to refer to non-Jews as dogs in a contemptuous manner. But that can hardly be the reference here. It is more likely in view of what follows that Paul is using the term to refer to Jews, or rather to some specific kinds of Jews. It has been objected that it would not have been comprehensible if Paul had used an anti-Gentile term in this kind of way as an anti-Jewish term: it would be as unlikely as that an Australian would denounce fellow-Australians as 'pommie bastards' (which is said to be an Australian term of abuse for the English). The point is debatable. If the context showed that a person was talking about Australians, then it would be possible to use the phrase to imply 'they are pommie bastards themselves rather than the English'. Paul is going to say in a moment that Christians are the true circumcision, not the Jews, and so it is quite likely that he could also say that Gentiles are not the [real] dogs, but (some of) the Jews are. But why use the term 'dogs'? To the Jews dogs were unclean animals. They thought that the uncircumcised Gentiles were religiously unclean, and by turning the term back upon them, Paul may be indicating that Jews who reject the message of the cross are 'unclean'.

Second, they are *those who do nothing but harm*. Literally Paul says 'evil workers'. In this context the word cannot refer to people doing immoral or wicked actions. Two other possibilities arise. First, it might refer to people who performed various good works whether to gain a good standing with God or as a way of showing that they had a good standing with him. Paul would then be saying that their good works are in fact evil. But this would be a very unusual use of language. The second possibility is that it refers to persons engaged in missionary work. The related term 'fellow-workers' is used by Paul in this sense (2.25; 4.3; Rom. 16. 3, 9, 21), and he uses 'workers' for the rival missionaries who were his opponents in II Cor. 11.13. Then 'evil workers' means people who carry out missionary work that Paul regards as misguided and evil in its effects.

Third, they are the people *who insist on mutilation*. This word can only be a rather vicious pun on 'circumcision' (the two words are similar in Greek: *peritomē* and *katatomē*). So we are dealing with people who practise circumcision or advocate it for other people. A reference to Jews is most likely. But Paul regards what they are doing as bad.

All this suggests most strongly that Paul is thinking of people who might come as missionaries to Philippi and encourage the Gentile members of the church to be circumcised. That such people existed we know from Galatians, which is a sustained polemic against such people in churches where they had already got a hold on some members of the church. No other explanation is so simple or so well-supported.

3.3   Paul's objection to them sprang out of his understanding of the gospel. What put people in the right with God was faith in Jesus, that and nothing more. It followed that Gentile believers were as much the people of God as were Jews who believed in Jesus. Paul would appear to have gone even further and denied that Jews who refused to believe in Christ were members of God's people. For in Paul's eyes what put a person in the right with God was faith in Jesus, and where this was lacking, then the physical act of circumcision was of no value. In fact, for Paul faith in Jesus meant that physical circumcision was a matter of indifference. True circumcision – the spiritual reality to which the physical rite testified – was a matter of the heart. And therefore the Christian church could boldly claim that its members were *the circumcision* (i.e. the circumcised people) in the proper sense of the term, even if there was nothing outward to show it. In a Jewish context this meant, 'We are truly God's people'; and it carried the implication that people who did not believe in Jesus were not truly God's people. Rom. 9–11 makes it perfectly clear that Paul saw the Jews of his day who did not believe in the Messiah as people who were misguidedly seeking God in the wrong kind of way – and so failing to find him. So, while Paul still believed that God had called 'Israel' originally to be his people, he felt that the Jews of his time who did not believe in Jesus as the Messiah had cut themselves off from Israel, but that in time there would be a fresh turning by his people to Jesus. Here, however, his point is not so much the negative one, that Jews who do not believe in Jesus are no longer God's people, but rather the positive one that Gentiles who believe in Jesus thereby do belong to God's people and do not need to be circumcised in addition.

What are the characteristics, then, of God's people?

First, they *worship* God. Here Paul is really talking about giving service to God. This was expressed in OT times by the religious ritual performed in the temple where sacrifices were offered to God and he was the object of praise and prayer by his people. Needless to say, this worship was closely linked with other forms of service, expressed in obedience to God's commands for ordinary life. God is thought of as a Lord who employs people to carry out his orders. Now his new people are to fulfil this role. They have become his people and they are therefore to serve him in appropriate ways. Paul saw himself as serving God 'in the gospel' (Rom. 1.9), and he encouraged the Christians at Rome to offer themselves to him as 'the worship offered by mind and heart' (Rom. 12.1). Here we see the two aspects of self-dedication to God: it corresponds to the offerings made in the temple and it requires service for God in the world.

But Paul adds here that Christians serve God *by the Spirit of God*. This phrase can simply indicate that they have the help of the Spirit in their efforts to serve God, just as the Spirit is said to help them in their prayers (Rom. 8.26). But there is probably more to it. Undoubtedly by the time he wrote this verse Paul already had developed the contrast between the law and faith which emerges a couple of verses later. Now in Rom. 2.29 Paul comments that true circumcision is a matter of the heart, not of a physical operation, and that it happens 'in the Spirit, not in the letter' (cf. Rom. 7.6). This contrast between the physical action and actions in the Spirit is probably present here. Paul is thinking of that inward, real service to God which is not a matter of external fulfilment of the requirements of the law but of a response of the whole person inspired by the Spirit. It is the new obedience which is in mind.

Second, Christians put their *pride... in Christ Jesus*. This means that Christians, like everybody else, find things in which they can rejoice and with which they can in a way identify themselves. A football supporter is proud of his football team (especially when it wins, but even sometimes when it loses), and such pride may be misplaced if, for instance, the team is given to foul play. A person may also rejoice in his or her own achievements, like the footballer who prances about to tell all the world that he has just scored a decisive goal and who enjoys not only having accomplished it but also receiving the praise of the rest of the team and the crowd. And both of these forms of rejoicing can become arrogant, self-centred and self-satisfied. The Jews in Paul's time were in danger of rejoicing or exulting in their own works of the law. They might boast that they had done them, whereas other people had not. But for the Christian there is one ground for boasting and pride, and one only, Jesus Christ and his sacrifice on the cross. It is on that that we depend for our standing with God, and not on anything at all that we have done. So there is no place for personal pride, and this means that what is here called 'pride' is no longer arrogant or self-centred or exclusive. Pride is purged of its sinful elements.

PRIDE

Words translated by such English words as 'pride' and 'boasting' are common in Paul. Paul recognized that human beings often show pride in themselves or their own achievements or in other people and actions in which they have some kind of share – just as fans may be proud of their football team's prowess although they contribute nothing (except perhaps their cheers) to it. He accepted that on the human level people might legitimately feel proud of their achievements (Rom. 4.2). But he insisted that in the sight of God people were not so entitled. On the contrary they could boast only in Christ and his death on the cross (Gal. 6.14). But once Paul starts to talk in this way, it is apparent that the words are losing the sense of feeling any pride in one's personal achievement and are taking on more the sense of feeling exultant, joyful and happy over what somebody else has done which is for their good. So here the Christian believer exults in Christ, an attitude that is the exact opposite of pride or arrogance inspired by one's own achievements. And exultation about other people becomes more exultation in Christ because of them (1.26; 2.16). Christians can rejoice in what Christ does in and through them – but without a sense of arrogant pride.

Closely linked with this, third, is the absence of *confidence in the physical*. Paul is here thinking of things like circumcision, physical descent from Abraham, and other marks of the Jewish religion seen in outwardly keeping the law. People depended on them as the means of their salvation. But Paul had repudiated all of these as a Christian; there was nothing human on which to depend, but only what God had done.

The sad thing was that in theory the Jewish religion said the same. The religion of the OT Scriptures emphasized that God had called Israel, and that the people had to respond with faith and love – and humility. But Paul's belief was that the Jews of his day had turned the law of God into a means of salvation for themselves and they put their trust and confidence therefore in what they were doing in response to God's requirements instead of in what God had done for them. Would Paul perhaps have said that the Jews did not believe in

Jesus as the Messiah because they did not feel the need for a Messiah to save them?

3.4 Then Paul proceeds to explain by personal example just what this confidence in physical things might mean. He is doing two things. First, he is showing the kind of things in which people could put their confidence. And, second, he is demonstrating that he himself had as good, if not better, grounds for such confidence than anybody else. He is going to show that in his own case they did him no good, and he had now come to regard them as utterly worthless; if so, it followed that the same must be true of any other Jew, for there would be few who could surpass Paul in his catalogue of Jewish qualifications and achievements. Paul is thus prepared for the sake of his argument to indulge in what might be called 'boasting'; he is prepared to say, 'Anything you can do, I can do better' – simply in order to be able to go on and say, 'But since I regard anything I can do as worthless, it follows that your achievements are worthless too, and you should regard them as such.'

3.5 There are seven items in the list:

(a) He had been *circumcised on* the *eighth day*. That is to say, he had undergone the ritual at birth on the precise day laid down in the law for the purpose. If, therefore, anything depended a person being able to say 'I'm better than you because I was circumcised earlier in life,' Paul could say that he had been circumcised as soon as was legally possible. He was no convert to Judaism, circumcised in adulthood. His parents had observed the law meticulously.

But the accent is on what happened, rather than on the day. The significance is that the Jewish law prescribed that every male Israelite had to undergo this surgical act, which was carried out as a religious ritual. Whatever its origins, it had become a distinctive, visible mark that a person belonged to Israel. If a person failed to be circumcised, the divine promises were ineffective in their case. Even if other nations performed the same ritual, it still lost none of its effectiveness as the essential mark of a Jew.

(b) He was *an Israelite by race*. This is a way of saying that he was native-born into God's people, and was not a convert from another nation. He could take pride and put confidence in the position in which he had been placed, and which could be attributed to a divine predestination of himself to be a member of the elect people.

(c) He belonged to the *tribe of Benjamin*. This means that he belonged to a family which could trace its pedigree, and which had an illustrious past. Benjamin was one of the two faithful tribes; it had stayed with Judah when the other tribes broke away after the death of Solomon and for a time turned apostate. Here, then, Paul is taking the position of the person who thinks that the illustrious history of one's family before one is born counts for something in the sight of God and man.

(d) He was *a Hebrew born and bred*. That is to say his parents were Hebrews and they brought him up as a Hebrew. This term probably refers to one of two groups that could be distinguished in the first century, the Hebrews and the Hellenists (cf. Acts 6.1). The latter were Jews who as a result of emigration or upbringing in other lands spoke Greek as their main language. The former were those who belonged to Judaea and as a consequence spoke the Jewish language; although the word 'Hebrew' was used for them, it was in fact a related language, Aramaic, which they spoke. With the language there went a life-style and a way of thinking. The differences must not be exaggerated, and we certainly cannot draw a rigid line between the two groups, but it is fair to say that the Aramaic-speakers tended to be more traditional-Jewish in their ways, while the Hellenistic Greek-speaking Jews were more open to non-Jewish culture. Back in the second century in Jerusalem itself the Hellenistic institution of the gymnasium was welcomed by some and fiercely attacked by other Jews. That was typical.

(e) Then come three phrases all introduced in the same way in the original Greek with the word 'in respect of' – the law, zeal and righteousness. First, *in my practice of the law a Pharisee*. Here Paul picks up the well-known fact that the most assiduous devotion to the law was found among the Pharisees. The precise identity and nature of the Pharisaic movement is surprisingly obscure, but at least one fact stands out clearly. The Pharisees were concerned that ordinary Israelites should keep the law meticulously, and therefore they were concerned, through the 'teachers of the law', to spell out in detail just what that meant. They are often thought to have made the law more difficult to keep by expanding its requirements – and certainly Jesus chided them for this. But their aim was a positive one. People could not be expected to keep the law if they did not know how it applied to their lives in detail, and therefore it was necessary to clarify it as precisely as possible. Inevitably this led to the danger of a pettifogging legalism, where nothing was left to imagination or good sense, but all was spelled out in tedious detail and precise obedience was required. But enthusiasm for the law as God's perfect revelation of his will lay at the bottom of it. And to this Paul subscribed. If religious devotion could be shown by keeping the requirements of God expressed in the law, then Paul was in the forefront.

3.6 Second, there was *zeal for religion*. Here we have another important word. It has given us the term 'Zealot' to denote somebody who has a passionate concern for some cause. When the word was used in Jewish circles, it had a religious sense and referred to an overwhelming passion for the cause of God and a determination to stamp out his enemies. It was an enthusiasm for God expressed in intolerance for his enemies and even in taking up arms against them. The archetypal 'zealot' was Phinehas who killed on the spot an Israelite who had taken a Midianite wife and adopted her religion (Num. 25, especially v. 11; Ps. 106.28–31). The Maccabean heroes stood in the same succession as they warred against those who tried to impose pagan religion and customs in Judaea. And now Paul saw his own crusade against the first Christians in the same way. Other people might feel passionately that the Christians were blaspheming against God; it was Paul who took action against them as far afield from Jerusalem as Damascus.

Finally, in this catalogue Paul makes the (to us) astounding claim that he was *by the law's standard of righteousness without fault*. He means at the very least that so far as outward observance of the many requirements of the law could be measured, nobody could raise a finger against him and accuse him of any shortcoming. He had a conscience that did not trouble him. No doubt he is saying this from the point of view of his Pharisaic past; looking back as a Christian on what he did then, he was conscious that his behaviour carried a different verdict. His conduct had been far from blameless, as he indicates, for example, in I Cor. 15.9 where he says that he was not fit to be an apostle because he had persecuted the church. However, that is not the point that Paul develops here. He is not talking about the sinfulness or otherwise of his conduct in the light of his later experience as a Christian. He is simply piling up the evidence that would appeal to a Jewish audience, showing that by the highest standards of attainment he was fully entitled to confidence in his position and his achievements. And in a moment he will bring the whole pile of cards crashing down, not by saying that he was in fact a guilty sinner (true though that was) but by saying that all these apparently good things in fact count for nothing.

3.7   It is to this point he comes in the startling metaphors of vv. 7–8. Here are the things that Jews regarded as the grounds of their confidence in God, the evidences that they were his people. Using the language of business and commerce, Paul says that they were *assets*, things that carried value and gave a person credit. And in a striking phrase he says that he has *written them off*. He no longer attaches any value to them. In fact, the Greek word used may go even further than the REB suggests: the older translation 'I count them as loss' brings out the force of the expression in that Paul may have regarded them as actual liabilities, things that could cause him loss. For it is possible that possession of all these things could in fact lead a person into a false sense of security and give the impression that all was well spiritually when in fact the position was dire.

What led Paul to this revaluation of his religious assets? It was *because of Christ*. On account of what he had come to know about Christ Paul came to see that the things which mattered to him formerly had ceased to be of value.

3.8a   But before pursuing this thought it is necessary to look at v. 8, which is a kind of correction and expansion of what has just been said. Here Paul says three things.

First, he expands the scope of his statement from *all such assets* to *everything*. It is not clear whether Paul is simply saying 'none of the things I have mentioned is excluded' or implying that there may be further things which he considered valuable other than those which he has listed. In any case, he is emphasizing that nothing matters in the question of where one places one's ultimate confidence except Christ.

Perhaps this was the basis for Martin Luther's lines:

> And though they take our life,
> Goods, honour, children, wife –
> Yet is their profit small.

Nevertheless, here we need to proceed carefully. Suppose that we do include all the other human assets that a person may have. There is surely no sense in which a Christian would consider these valueless and even as liabilities: to say this of one's wife or children is surely false! At most, these things are relatively less valuable than 'the city of God' or Christ. The Christian values them, but he values Christ far, far more. What Paul is getting at is rather making human assets into a basis for religious confidence and boasting. Two kinds of religion are being contrasted. Paul is not here in the asceticism game, in which a person ceases to be concerned about people and possessions in this world – for these are God's gifts to us, and we are stewards or managers of them for his sake.

Second, Paul switches the tenses of the verb he uses. If v. 7 refers to an attitude which he had developed in the past, this verse indicates that his attitude has not changed and continues to be the same. There is no going back on the new outlook that he has come to have as a Christian.

Third, Paul expresses his attitude to his religious assets even more forcefully by saying that he counts them as *so much rubbish*. Here the REB is weak. Paul's language could not be stronger, for the word he uses here was employed to refer to excrement or to the remains of a feast, decaying and smelly food, gathered up and used to feed animals 'Garbage' gives about the right sense. Placing the basis of his religious confidence and pride in these things has now become downright unpleasant to his mind. He could not express his revulsion any more plainly.

Fourth, Paul again makes it clear that this change in his attitude came about through Jesus Christ. Three points emerge here.

(a) Paul had in a real sense written off many of these assets. He was no longer recognized as a Pharisee, and he could no longer claim that he kept the law in all its minute details. (He would say of course that he really kept the essence of the law which remains in force for God's people at all times, and which Jesus summed up as total love for God and for other people.) So the claims which he had made earlier in life were now in tatters.

(b) But more important was the fact that the coming of Jesus had rendered these claims to religious status obsolete. As Paul explains in Rom. 3, God has now provided a new way for people to get right with him, through the coming of Jesus and his sacrificial death. By this action God has shown that the alternative way of getting right with him no longer works. It is in fact questionable whether it ever did work. There is a good case that what mattered in the OT and Judaism was the love of God which made the Jews his people and to which they were to respond with faith and love. Once they began to depend upon the outward signs of making that response and to place confidence in them, they had missed the point.

(c) However, the point that Paul develops here is rather that he has abandoned the old sources of religious confidence because he has found something better and more satisfying in Christ. He talks here of *the gain of knowing Christ Jesus* [as] *my Lord*. If we try to unpack this idea. it seems to be that Paul had discovered a new experience which he calls 'knowing Christ' and he found this experience so overwhelmingly wonderful that it became the centre of his concern. We may say that Paul is talking in human terms about the relative value of different assets to their owner. He compares the value of having the religious privileges of the pious Jew with the experience of knowing Christ, and he says that there is simply no comparison between the two: confidence in the physical is completely over-shadowed by knowing Christ.

It may appear to be a slightly curious argument, because it seems to be couched in terms of what a person finds most satisfying, instead of in terms of what is ultimately true or what is actually effective in bringing salvation. But Paul would doubtless have replied that he was in fact comparing the full revelation of God's saving purpose in Christ with the mistaken route followed by Judaism, and saying that the former was not only the true way but also the better and more satisfying way.

Note that the knowledge is of Christ as *Lord*. This phrase echoes the early Christian confession that people probably made when they were baptized: Jesus [Christ] is Lord (2.11; Rom. 10.9; I Cor. 12.3). There are thus two elements in Paul's experience.

The first is the acceptance of Jesus as Lord. That means sharing in and accepting the verdict that God the Father passed upon Jesus when he raised him from the dead and exalted him. It is to say that the person who had been crucified, apparently as a criminal, in deepest degradation, and who was therefore despised by people in general, was actually the most important person in the universe, sharing the authority and sovereignty of God. To be a Christian meant that one accepted the status given to Jesus by God. What unbelieving Jews did was to deny that Jesus had this status. Christians accepted Jesus as Lord – and therefore understood his commands as having all the authority of God behind them. We note the obvious link-up with 2.9–11.

The second element was that Paul *knew* Jesus in this way. This means something more than simply recognizing the status of Jesus. The meaning of the phrase is debated, but a personal relationship, akin to that in which we might claim to know a human person, is indicated. Jesus had spoken personally to Paul at his conversion, and Paul believed that he continued to do so from time to time. Therefore

Paul as an individual was known to God (cf. Gal 4.9) and knew God. It is this individual relationship to Jesus which Paul has in mind. And just as knowing some people is a rich experience by comparison with knowing others who are less attractive, so knowing Jesus was for Paul the highest of relationships. (We may compare how we find some human beings more attractive to know than others, whether as friends or as lover, not only because they also show interest in us but also because they are interesting, stimulating, understanding, etc.)

This explanation is more probable than others which try to understand knowing Christ simply in terms of the OT idea that knowing God is the same as keeping his commandments or in terms of the mystical union found in some ancient religions.

3.8b We can now go on to the fuller statement which Paul gives here and which in a sense explains more clearly what is involved in knowing Christ. It is put in terms of aims which Paul has, just as a human being may speak of wanting to get to know somebody better. Paul gives two such aims, and qualifies the second at some length.

The first is that of *gaining Christ*. This is an unusual phrase, not used elsewhere by Paul. It could mean that he wants to have Christ as an asset, in contrast to the assets which he has given up; there could be a play on words pointing in this direction. Or there might be a link back to 1.21 where Paul says that dying is gain; does he mean here that he wants to enter into the new world which lies beyond death so that there he can experience knowing Christ to the full? (The next phrase might also point in this direction.) Or we may take the word in the sense of acquiring something, as a person might gain the world (Mark 8.36), or win converts (I Cor 9.19). But it is difficult to see how Paul might hope to 'acquire' Christ. So perhaps we need to take the word in a weak sense. Can it possibly mean simply 'to get to know Christ even more', or does it refer to a fulfilled purpose: that Paul gave up everything for the sake of his present experience of already having a relationship with Christ? Then it could refer not to any sort of effort to 'win' Christ for himself, but to his giving up of his religious privileges for the sake of 'getting' Christ in their place as something (or rather somebody) far more worth having? This seems to be the most satisfactory explanation.

3.9 If that is the case, then the next phrase must be also be taken as referring to an existing situation. *Finding myself in union with him* is the other part of Paul's aim. The phrase could in fact be taken of a future aim, yet to be realized, namely that when the end of the world comes, and everybody is brought to judgment and is 'discovered' openly, then Paul will be discovered to be *in union with him* and therefore a member of the saved, elect group who are not condemned but rather accepted by God. This interpretation takes 'discovered' almost to be a technical term (it is certainly an unusual one) for a future 'uncovering' of a person's real situation. However, the last part of v. 9 suggests that a present situation may be in mind, and this is confirmed by Paul's language elsewhere (Rom. 5.1) which makes it clear that Christians are already 'in union with Christ' and already justified. Therefore, we propose tentatively that what Paul wanted was to be in this new relationship here and now. In other words, 'found' refers to the unveiling in the future of a relationship that already exists.

In the remainder of v. 9 the significance of being in union with Christ is spelled out in detail. The effect of this relationship is that a person has a new 'righteousness'. Paul explains it by a contrast which involves two elements:

righteousness of my own	based on the law
righteousness given by God	from faith in Christ

Here we see that Paul thinks of righteousness as a state or quality which may be conferred by God or which people may try to secure by their own efforts. The former is *based on the law*, by which Paul must mean by doing the works required by the law; the latter comes through faith, by which Paul must mean accepting what God has done for us in Christ.

It is difficult to avoid the impression that here Paul is thinking of the way in which a person might claim to establish their own position in relation to God by keeping the law. He uses this contrast to explain more clearly that the new relationship with Christ brings righteousness as a gift from God.

Three points need to be made in explanation. First, *righteousness* is a word that in English expresses a quality. In biblical thinking the idea is more of a relationship, in which a person is accepted by God as being in good standing. God regards the person as being free of guilt, as innocent of any sin – despite the fact that the person was and is a sinner.

Second, this happens for people who are *in union with Christ*, literally *in Christ*. This very difficult, but extremely important phrase, signifies that a person is so closely joined to Christ that what is true of Christ is true of the person; in particular, because Christ made himself 'sin' (taking what was ours upon himself), he can share with us his righteousness (II Cor. 5.21).

Third, this situation is brought about by *faith*. When a person trusts and commits him/herself to God, then the effect is to bring about this close relationship. The relationship is probably one of *faith in Christ*, as REB translates the phrase.

> However, there is a powerful school of interpretation which suggests that this particular phrase refers to the faith shown by Christ himself. This view is improbable.

3.10 We now have a further statement of purpose which is rather loosely attached to what preceded. It could be simply a reformulation of the purpose expressed in vv. 8b–9. It is more likely to follow on from those verses and to indicate Paul's continuing purpose and aim as a Christian. The theme of knowing Christ is now expanded by two further phrases. Thus there are three points here.

First, the aim of the Christian life is to *know Christ*. This suggests that knowing Christ is an ongoing experience which deepens and matures like the experience of getting to know any other person.

CHRIST THE ONLY SAVIOUR

Some people think that the Christian religion is basically about one way to final salvation and immortality, alongside which there can be other ways which are equally valid. They want to affirm that there are (at least) two ways of salvation, one for Christians via Christ and one for Jews (and others) via their religion. It is doubtful whether this view can be upheld without contradicting Paul.

Here Paul displays an exclusivism over against the Jewish way of salvation which can be universalized over against any other form of religiosity which bypasses Christ. Paul appears to state quite plainly that Christ relativizes even Judaism, which of all religions has the best claim to be the alternative route to God. Even if he puts his point in strong language because of the opposition which he was facing, this was his settled opinion, and it is highly significant that he says the same kind of thing with tears in Rom. 9–11 as he thinks of the way in which so many of his

contemporaries were cutting themselves off from God by rejecting Christ. Paul held to this position despite considerable
pressure to think otherwise; it was a thought which filled him
with grief and with a longing that, if it was possible, he himself
might lose salvation in order that his compatriots might gain it.

This passage also shows that Paul's religion was one in which
Christ was not simply a way to a final goal. Rather, the experience
of knowing Christ here and now was in itself part of the goal. The
person who is not a Christian but follows some other route to the
goal fails to experience salvation here and now.

The question of the ultimate fate of those who have never heard
the gospel (or who have heard it imperfectly or have been inocu-
lated against it by witnessing the lovelessness of Christians) is a
different question that should not be confused with the question
of deliberately rejecting Christ.

Second, knowing Christ involves experiencing *the power of his
resurrection*. This must mean the power of God which raised Jesus
and which can have a similar life-giving effect in our lives. Paul's
doctrine here is twofold. On the one hand, he undoubtedly has in
mind the power which raises dead bodies and transforms them to be
spiritual bodies, like the body of Christ. On the other hand, he
thinks of this transformation as a process which has already started,
so that, in the midst of the gradual decay of the human body during
the course of life, a resurrection body is already forming, and this
means that a new spiritual and ethical life is growing in us. Thus the
force of Paul's phrase is both ethical and physical. The life of Christ
is revealed here and now in our mortal bodies in the new life of the
Christian.

Third, at the same time the Christian knows or experiences what
it is *to share his sufferings*. This phrase is very close to what Peter says
in I Peter 4.13 where he tells Christians who are persecuted that they
are sharers in the sufferings of Christ. Thus the sufferings which
Christians bear as Christians are part of the sufferings in which
Christ shared, and they bring them into closer union with Christ.
They are the result of the opposition of the world to God and to his
will, but they are also what Christ and Christians have to bear in
order to overcome the opposition and to neutralize it. Suffering with
Christ is the lot of the Christian witness.

What Paul is saying is that the Christian life has this twofold
character of being ready to share in suffering for the sake of the

gospel and of experiencing the power that raised Christ from the dead right in the midst of it. Power and weakness belong together; life and death are co-ordinated experiences. The Christian life is one of crucifixion and resurrection, not of crucifixion followed by resurrection, but of resurrection in the midst of crucifixion; we are 'as dying and behold we live' (II Cor. 6.9).

Paul sums this aspect of Christian experience up in a further phrase. He talks of *growing conformity with his death, in hope of somehow achieving the resurrection from the dead*. This is further explanation of what he has already said. What new things does it add to what has been said?

To live *in growing conformity with his death* suggests not that Paul was thinking of martyrdom but that he saw the Christian life as following the kind of pattern that Jesus showed in his attitude to his death. We have seen something of this in 2.5–11 where the major motif was the willingness of Jesus to surrender, or not to use, what was his by right, to take the role of a servant and to endure the humiliation of death on the cross. The attitudes which he showed throughout his earthly life were summed up and most clearly expressed in the way in which he died. Similarly in II Cor. 8.9 Paul spoke of the grace of Jesus seen in his willingness to become poor so that other people might become rich. Again, the element of his obedience to God is found here in 2.5–11 and in Gal. 4. There are references to his meekness and gentleness. The concept of dying for the sake of others – of being, in the familiar phrase 'the man for others' – sums up one aspect of this. And thus we see that there was an attitude of Jesus to God and to other people which was expressed in the way that he died. For Paul Christian growth meant sharing this attitude more and more.

3.11 The goal of it all was to attain the resurrection. The *somehow* may suggest that the achievement of the goal was in some doubt. But this is highly unlikely for Paul; his strong sense of assurance elsewhere and even later in this chapter make it most improbable that he had any real doubt about his future. The uncertainty may be an expression of humility. Or it may reflect uncertainty about the route to the destination. Paul did not know whether he would die before Christ returned, in which case he would hope for resurrection, or whether he would still be alive, in which case he would look forward to the heavenly meeting described in I Thessalonians 4. But he did know that the goal he desired was to be with the risen Christ.

Possibly there is a contrast with the hope of the resurrection held by the Jews and mentioned in Acts 24:15. If so, the underlying agenda is to stress that the hope of resurrection depends upon Christ and not upon holding some kind of hope based on the Jewish law and style of life.

THE CRUCIFORM LIFE

This passage is significant for its positive expression of the Christian life in terms of personal relationship with Christ. It fits in with a repeated emphasis of Paul on the need for a so-called cruciform life – one whose pattern is the cross.

The Christian way is not an easy option. For Paul it was of incomparable worth, involving what he saw as a personal knowledge of Christ. But this was possible only if believers are prepared at the same time to take the way of the cross, which means saying No to selfish desires and being prepared for opposition and rejection, possibly even martyrdom, at the hands of the powers of evil opposed to Christ.

The Christian life, then is a paradoxical combination of crucifixion and resurrection, of weakness and strength, of suffering with Christ and enjoying fellowship with him.

Put in these abstract terms, it may not seem too easy to preach. Seeing it incorporated in Jesus himself, in Paul and in Christians like Epaphroditus, may help to make it vivid and real.

Christian maturity
3.12–16

This section develops the thought that, although Paul has certain aims in his Christian life, he has not yet achieved them, but he is still intent on them. He is concerned with people in the church who think of themselves as 'mature' and urges them not to fall back in any way but to press on further, just as he is doing. In short, there is no point at which the Christian can sit back and say that the goal has been reached; A. M. Hunter quotes the Scots farm-labourer who said: 'Him that has aye something ayont [beyond] need never be weary.'

Paul's concern is to impress on his readers that there is 'something ayont' towards which they should be moving.

3.12   Paul begins by saying that he has not *already achieved this*. What is *this*? (The word is absent from the Greek.) It obviously cannot refer back to what immediately precedes, the resurrection from the dead.

> This interpretation might be possible if Paul had in mind some first-century Christians who claimed that the resurrection had happened already, and that they had themselves been resurrected. After all, what Paul says about dying and rising with Christ in Rom 6 might be misunderstood in that way.

Rather, as the second half of the verse confirms, Paul is referring to the whole of the experience of knowing Christ as described in v. 10. He is, then, saying that he has not completely achieved his aim.

The next phrase is meant to clarify what has just been said. Paul says that he has *not yet reached perfection*. The explanation is no clearer than the original statement, largely because Paul is here using a word which may have been familiar to his readers, but not to us. That it was familiar to them may be guessed from v. 15. The verb is not used by Paul elsewhere. He does refer to Christians who are *mature* in I Cor. 2.6; and he refers to this state as a Christian goal in Eph. 4.13; Col. 1.28; 4.12. Part of the problem is whether he is using the word to refer to a specific category of Christians with fairly precise characteristics or in a more vague way to refer to people who are relatively more mature than others. The latter is the more likely.

So it appears that Paul is emphasizing that the aim expressed in v. 10 remains an aim which he has not completely achieved – and which perhaps one can never say one has totally achieved. His position is that of somebody who is strenuously making progress. He *presses on* – the picture now is that of an athlete continuing to run in a race to the end or of a hunter who does not give up on a long trek while stalking his prey. He has an aim in view which is to get hold of that for which Christ took hold of him. (The picture may be that of an army pursuing the defeated enemy in order to capture spoil, Ex. 15.9.) There is a play on words here. Christ has already taken full possession of Paul; Paul in turn wants full possession of Christ.

3.13–14   The renewed appeal to *my friends* is intended to emphasize the point which Paul now states yet again and to ensure that they see that it has an application to them. He is concerned to make it as clear as possible that in no sense has he fully grasped Christ.

Why is he so emphatic? Possibly some people thought that he had become 'mature', and he had to put them straight on the matter. But more likely there were other people who claimed that they were mature, and he wants in effect to say, 'If I haven't got there yet, no more have you. All of us together must press on further.'

What then is his position? The race metaphor which was hinted at in v. 12 is now fully expressed. The picture is that of a foot race in which the runners ran in a stadium towards a marker in hope of winning a prize. It was essential to run towards the mark and not to look back longingly at some other destination or turn aside from the track. The race demanded concentration on the one aim, to reach the marker first. With Paul the competitive element in the picture is absent; the point is that each and every runner must strive with all their might to reach the winning post so as to gain the prize. So Paul emphasizes:

(a) *Forgetting what is behind*. The previous goals in life, described in vv. 5–6, have to be put aside. Longing after them will in fact divert the runner from reaching the goal. The thought can obviously be widened out. For people attach the same false value to good works of whatever kind as establishing their own reputation with God, whereas God chooses to accept us solely on the basis of his grace. Phil. 3 does indeed say No to human religion.

(b) *Straining towards what lies ahead*. The picture is still that of the runner who strives towards the goal that can be seen in front. But this is metaphor. The application is doubtless to the prospect of communion with Christ. There is a goal to be achieved. Note, then, that here there is a place for human effort and even work. How then does it stand over against that which Paul repudiates? Even if everything depends on divine grace, yet here there is a zeal for religion which rivals that of Judaism in its intensity. Why is this effort right and that effort wrong? Clearly Paul does believe in religious effort and religious enthusiasm, but he sees it as the effort to go in what he now sees as God's way. The effect of Christianity is to set a person free from wrongly-directed effort, not from effort itself. Was Paul conscious of any apparent contradiction between the two?

(c) *Press towards the finishing line*. This is an unusual phrase for the goal in a race, and it simply continues the metaphor in the previous phrase. Perhaps it is meant to stress that there is a conclusion to the race; it doesn't go on for ever!

(d) There is a *heavenly prize* to be won. Here the metaphor does break down. In a normal race, as Paul knew, only one person was the winner (I Cor. 9.24), but he probably also recognized that there was more than one heavenly crown (II Tim. 4.8). So here he says that he longs to win the crown. But he encourages other people to do so, and he says nothing to suggest that only one of them would be successful. The prize is associated with God's upward call. This means that God calls us to a crown, or to a path which leads to a crown.

That could be seen as a reward for faithful pilgrimage, for successful runners. Can we altogether get rid of this element of the appeal to (doubtless) 'sanctified' ambition? Can we avoid the idea of effort leading to success? Has the rat-race of Judaism been abolished, only to be replaced by another of equal intensity? How can we avoid the false ideas and ambitions that can so easily be associated with the race concept?

The call comes *in Christ Jesus*. Here the phrase goes in effect with the verb inherent in the phrase: God calls us in and through Jesus, i.e. through the gospel message about him. Christ is the channel, the means, the instrument used by God when he calls us.

3.15   The application is now made. Paul has described his way of life as a Christian, and the accent is on the fact that he is still en route; he has not arrived but has still a distance to travel, and effort is needed. Now he addresses those who are *mature*, and the form of words indicates that he includes himself in their number. It is the language of exhortation and appeal, in which the preacher numbers himself with his audience. Now Paul has already said in v. 12 that he has not yet reached perfection; here he uses the corresponding adjective to describe others and himself. Perhaps then he means something more like 'all those among us who think of themselves as mature – and not necessarily all of us would use the term (I for one would not) – must have this way of thinking'. There were people who did think of themselves as 'mature'. Paul says: Not even I think of myself as fully mature but as 'on the way', and I behave correspondingly. So you too must think of yourselves: you may be more mature than others, but you are still on the way and have some distance to go. You have not yet arrived.

Then comes the strange comment. If people do not have the

attitude of mind they should have, God will make this fact plain to them. How this will happen Paul does not say. He simply comments that it will happen. To be sure, people can close their ears to what God has to say about them. Was Paul thinking of the effect of prophetic messages in the church, which might reveal a person's mind (I Cor. 14.24f.)? Certainly Paul believes that God can show people where they think differently from what they ought to think as Christians, when they have false ambitions.

3.16   Finally, he says that our conduct must be consistent with what we have already attained. This is put very succinctly in the Greek. In practice it would seem to mean that the Christian is to go on living by that Christian level of insight which has already been reached. The Christian is not to go backwards to a lower level of insight. And in particular this means not going back to the false belief that the works of the law are what matter. This incidentally suggests that the danger had not yet corrupted the church

CHRISTIAN PERFECTION

The term 'perfect' has played a significant role in Methodist theology ever since John Wesley claimed that 'Christian perfection' or 'perfect love' was the goal which Christians can reach in this life, and that it can be attained by an act of faith similar to that involved in becoming a Christian. The term 'perfect' is used in the NT to describe the goal of the Christian life. Paul envisages Christians being 'flawless and without blame' when Christ returns (1.10). But it seems that the term 'perfect' was also used as a self-description by some Christians whom Paul would not have regarded as 'perfect'. Indeed, we might say that the word has the characteristic oddity that it may be possible for one person to use it of another person, but it is not appropriate for people to use it about themselves. I may be able to recognize that X is a mature Christian, perhaps the most mature one I know, but if X says 'I am mature', then we shall be tempted to see here a possibly arrogant attitude which is inconsistent with the claim!

Nevertheless, the question still arises as to whether the language is appropriate. Theologians in the Calvinist tradition are most uneasy with Wesley at this point! It can be argued:

98

1. The terminology is biblical, and therefore can be accepted as valid. There is a proper use for it.

2. Wesley's rather harassed efforts to define precisely what was and what was not included in 'perfection' indicate that a precise formulation is not possible. But the general concept of a mind or heart that is dominated by love and filled with Christ expresses the ideal adequately.

3. Used in this way, the concept is not basically different from the concept of sanctification found in Reformed theology.

4. Wesley's view was that there was a 'state' of perfection which might be attained instantaneously by an act of faith – a sort of 'second blessing'; this is not justified by NT teaching. The 'path to perfection' is more one of gradual process – although there can be significant crises and forward leaps!

5. Paul avoids any suggestion that there is an identifiable group of people in the church who are 'mature' or an identifiable list of characteristics of a 'mature' person so that readers could measure themselves against them and see if they qualified. Rather, Paul simply says, if you think you are mature, then take the same attitude as I do: regard yourselves as being still on the way.

Two ways of life
3.17–4.1

3.17   Paul sums up what he has just said in an appeal to the readers to join together in following his example. The urgency of the appeal is emphasized by his addressing them as *my friends*. At the same time the appeal is also one for unity in the church (*join together*). Evidently Paul fears the danger of a split with some people going his way and others following a different one. He wants the church to be united in following his way.

The point is carried further by reference to other people who live in the same kind of way. Evidently there are people who do accept Paul's gospel and his aim of seeking to know Christ. These will be members of the church in Philippi, and visitors like Timothy or the returning Epaphroditus in whose lives the Pauline gospel could be seen at work. Therefore, there were examples ready to hand for the Christians to follow.

THE PLACE OF EXAMPLE

The power of example cannot be over-emphasized. It is true that we have not seen Christ for ourselves and that we cannot always easily visualize what his life-style was. Therefore we look for human examples to follow. Young people especially look up to those just a little older than themselves and imitate them in what they do. The group slightly ahead of us in age can be just as influential, if not more influential than our peers. Therefore a great responsibility lies upon us, and the old principle about not acting in a way that sets a wrong example to a weaker brother needs to be reiterated. It is still important.

It requires considerable confidence for a Christian to tell others to follow his or her example. Paul is referring to his rejection of the works of the law and his dependence on Christ alone. There is no suggestion of personal pride here. Nor is there any suggestion that people must narrowly conform to a particular life-style; the appeal is on a broader basis than that.

3.18 For Paul the point was emphasized by the fact of other Christians who lived in a different way and who needed to be unmasked for what they really were. What is important is that Paul can speak of them as *enemies of the cross of Christ*. This is strong language. It could signify either that the people in question openly declared their antagonism to the message of the cross, or that their way of life was in effect antagonistic to it. The latter is the more likely in view of the reference to their *way of life*. They may not then have said in so many words that they were opposed to the cross, but Paul saw this as the implication of their behaviour. It is improbable that he was referring to non-Christians in general when he spoke in this way. The clear implication is that these people were liable to be taken as examples to follow by the Christians at Philippi; therefore they were people who presented themselves as Christians.

THE PROBLEM OF NOMINAL CHRISTIANS

For Paul mere attachment to the church or Christian profession was not an infallible indication of a person's true spiritual position. Not all who were in the church were necessarily what we might call 'friends of the cross'. And Paul was quite prepared to expose them openly for what they were.

This is clean contrary to a modern trend to accept everybody who claims to follow Christ for what they claim to be and to cast no doubts on their sincerity or the truth of their claim. A person may claim to be a Christian and yet follow a pattern of life that we might wish to say was opposed to the way of Christ, and yet we would not be allowed to question the sincerity of their Christian convictions. Thus a person who committed racial injustice and upheld, let us say, apartheid by the sword would have to be recognized as a sincere Christian because he claimed to follow Christ.

Doubtless, there are people who are sincere Christians and who have not realized the implications of their way of life. And surely such people need to be persuaded to see the incompatibility of their actions with their professed faith. But are there not also cases where a person claims to follow Christ and yet does not keep his commandments to such an extent that there is legitimate ground for questioning whether that person is a Christian, and trying to lead them to a genuine conversion?

Of course, we may be mistaken as to what is the Christian way and must allow for differences of opinion on problematic matters. Although I find it very difficult, for example, to see any other attitude than total abstinence with regard to alcohol as the right life-style for Christians, I have to recognize that other Christians do sincerely differ from me on this issue. On the other hand it is very hard for some of us to believe that people who live together but refuse to be joined in marriage are living a Christian life-style, even if others will try to assure us that we are wrong on this.

But, allowing for cases where there may be genuine difference of opinion as to the Christian way, it is still the case that there are ways of living such that Christians can only weep over those who are so deluded regarding the way of Christ that their life-style is incompatible with the cross.

3.19   Why did Paul weep over them? Because their path was *heading for destruction*. He was doubtless thinking of their ultimate fate at the day of judgment. For Paul the possibility of ultimate spiritual loss was very real. He knew of only one way to be found righteous at that day, and that was through being found in union with Christ (3.9). There was no other way. Paul could feel that if people lived in certain ways, this was a sign that they had turned their backs on salvation, and therefore he could feel the deepest sadness for them.

THE PROBLEM OF FINAL JUDGMENT

As with the problem of 'nominal Christians', so too this part of Paul's teaching is often regarded as unacceptable today. Many Christians today do not feel the concern that Paul felt over the ultimate fate of those who reject Christ. There are two reasons: First, they doubt whether there is such a thing as *destruction*, and they prefer to believe that in the providence of God all people will eventually find their way into his kingdom. This is certainly not the prima facie teaching of the NT. At the same time, it must be said equally firmly that the notion that anybody who has never heard the gospel is automatically excluded from any hope of heaven has a very dubious basis; it is people who reject Christ rather than people who have never heard of him who are threatened with destruction. If God is a God of mercy, it is surely right to believe that those who have not heard the gospel will be treated in the light of that fact. Shall not the judge of all the earth do right? Yet this does not take away the threat of destruction for those who are enemies of the cross. Granted that Paul's language is not to be taken literally (in the sense of never-ending bodily torment or the like), it is difficult to avoid the biblical concept that judgment faces those who reject divine love, and the church ought to take it far more seriously.

Second, it is arguable that the fate of eternal destruction is so awful to contemplate, that it would cause an intolerable pain and sadness to face up to it. To fear, for example, that some close member of one's family who is persisting in opposition to Christ is heading for destruction is too awesome to enable us to face any other part of life with equanimity, just as parents who are watching their child dying of cancer can think of little if anything else. Does God intend us to live with such a grim shadow over our lives?

For Paul it was a source of deep agony to see his fellow-Jews rejecting Christ and heading, as he believed, to destruction. This may well suggest to us that our complacency and lack of concern about people who are opposed to Christ is out of place, and that we should feel a far deeper concern than we do. A greater love for others in their need would lead the church to be more active in its evangelism and its concern for people who turn away from Christ.

These people are said to *make appetite their god*. This is a phrase which may mean no more than that they are ruled by self-interest and selfishness. But the reference is specifically to the body, and therefore the satisfaction of bodily desires, whether for food and drink or for sexual satisfaction, may be in mind. This would then be a straight case of people who prefer bodily comfort and enjoyment to the self-denial inherent in the way of the cross. Such people do exist, and such desires exist, though people may prefer to express the matter in terms that conceal its earthiness and selfishness.

However, in the present context another interpretation is possible, which is that these were people who took pride in their circumcision – and the other outward signs of Judaism. This may be the better solution to the problem, in that it produces a unity within the chapter and identifies the trouble-makers at the beginning of the chapter with this group.

They glory *in what should bring shame*. This again would fit in with a reference to physical desires that are in fact sordid. Here Paul would be thinking of gluttony, drunkenness and sexual promiscuity. That such sins existed in the Pauline churches is clear enough from I Corinthians 5, etc. Alternatively, the reference is to people who gloried in the signs of Judaism which Paul here goes so far as to call shameful.

Their minds are set on earthly things. The nearest parallel to this is Col. 3.2ff., where earthly things are placed in contrast to heavenly as the objects of human desire, and are linked with sinful desires which are explicitly catalogued. We have, therefore, people who think that a selfish and sinful way of life is compatible with the way of Christ. Or, again, Paul is thinking specifically of the human boasting in the outward signs of Judaism which he had repudiated at the beginning of the chapter.

3.20 Over against such people with their glorification of the earthly body and their miserable future Paul places those who have a heavenly future. Christians have their citizenship in heaven. That is to say, they belong to the equivalent of a human nation-state which is in heaven; the implication is that they are 'resident aliens' in another country to which they do not really belong (and therefore whose ways they do not adopt). But they follow the life-style of their native land and await the coming of a Deliverer from their home country who will rescue them from their exile and bring them home. The reference is plainly to the second coming or parousia of Jesus. The imagery is that of a visiting head of state, here probably regarded as a conqueror or invader who delivers those of his people who have fallen into captivity in a foreign land. But the imagery is not pressed, and it is quickly replaced by a different picture, that of Christ as the transformer.

But before we come to it, we note that the longing of Christians is centred on the coming of Jesus. They do have a forward look, and are not tied to the things of the present and the things all round them. They are not content with their present situation. They are like Paul who presses on toward the mark in the race because he wants to be united with Christ. So too Christians look forward eagerly to the coming of Christ.

3.21 And with good reason. For the life of the Christian in the body is one of frustration. The body is no doubt good and beautiful, but it is subject to all the pains and frustrations of life in a fallen world. It is prey to disease and disaster; it is slowly wearing away and becoming less and less efficient, and one day it will die, whether through decay or through sudden calamity; it is the seat of desires and passions that can bring about its own destruction. It has much good about it, but it is caught up in the cycle that terminates in death. Against all this the Christian believes in the possibility of the transformation of the body into something beautiful and incorruptible like the body of the risen Lord.

THE RESURRECTION OF THE BODY

It sounds like wishful thinking, totally unrealistic. You have only to go and look at a dead body, perhaps one that has been smashed up in a road accident, or worse still face the challenge of a body that has been literally vapourized in an explosion so that there is nothing left, and ask whether destruction can be undone. It's laughable. It's pathetic to imagine that there can be any reversal. You might also, of course, look at a dead bulb in the garden in the autumn, and then at the brilliantly coloured daffodil or tulip in the springtime that follows. You might think of the transformations that can take place within the physical world. And then ask whether anything comparable is possible in the spiritual world. If there is a God, can anything be too difficult for him? And if he has raised Jesus from the dead, can he not do the same again? 'Where is now thy victory, boasting grave?' Can we believe anything less?

That is the challenge Paul places before us. That is the implication of faith in Christ. He now exercises the power that God the Father once exercised upon him. He has the ultimate power over all things. He can do it.

4.1 Finally, Paul draws the consequence. In view of all this, they can be summoned *to stand firm in the Lord*. A wealth of ideas are packed together in this verse.

First, Paul's affection for his friends is expressed in a remarkably warm address to the recipients as the objects of his love and longing. He echoes 1.8, where he spoke of his longing for them, and 2.26, where he refers to Epaphroditus, and he describes them as the source of his joy (as in I Thess. 2.19) and crown; both of these expressions appear to look forward to the coming of the Lord Jesus when his people will meet him, and refer to the fact that Paul will be able to meet Jesus with joy because his missionary work has produced fruits. He will be able, in a manner of speaking, to 'wear' them just like the wreath of a victor at the games or the garland of honour that might be presented to a guest at a feast. Nevertheless, Paul describes them as being his joy and crown here and now; he is anticipating the happiness of the future occasion, and saying that the Philippians are already the source of his joy and of his confidence that he will not appear as it were empty-handed before his Master.

Second, Paul has in mind the threat to the readers from the people described in ch. 3 and gives them encouragement based on the promises contained in 3.20f.: Christians can look forward to the coming of Jesus and to the overthrow of the enemies of the cross. But if this hope is to be fulfilled and Paul's work is not to prove to have been in vain (cf. I Thess. 3.5), they must *stand firm* in their Christian faith (here Paul repeats the hope and the implicit command expressed in 1.27). The picture is of soldiers maintaining their position on the field of battle despite pressure to retreat. *To stand firm in the Lord* means that they can be strong on the basis of the power of the Lord to sustain them and through their trust in him.

Third, when Paul says, *This is what it means*, he is pointing forwards and preparing the way for the commands that will follow in the next part of the letter.

This verse thus has the character of a 'bridge' between one section of the letter and the next. It brings what has just been said to a conclusion, and it points forward to what is to follow. Many commentators and translations make it the last part of the section which covers ch. 3 (so REB, NIV; cf. I Cor. 15.58). But the language and ideas seem to belong more with the kind of teaching given in chs. 1, 2 and 4, and therefore it is likely that it is going on to draw a practical conclusion from the whole of what has preceded. Verses 2–10 in fact form the climax of the argument for the readers to live a life worthy of the gospel in unity and joyfulness.

It is worth noting against advocates of dismembering the letter that 4.1 would not follow on very naturally from the end of ch. 2 if ch. 3 were omitted. It is more probable that here Paul is resuming the 'thread' of the letter after the 'digression' in ch. 3.

Practical instructions for life in the church
4.2–9

We now have a series of very practical injunctions, such as are often found towards the end of a Pauline letter. They are concerned with:

1. Unity within the church between quarrelling members (4.2–3).
2. Joy in the Lord (4.4).
3. A spirit of sweet reasonableness (4.5).
4. Absence of anxiety and care through prayer (4.6–7).
5. High thinking based on moral standards and good behaviour based on church teaching and example (4.8–9).

This short list of commands at first sight does not show any clear structure and logic; it may seem rather like some of the material in the book of Proverbs, and we may be puzzled as to its direct relevance to the situation of the church. Sometimes at the end of a letter Paul gives a series of injunctions that are partly related to the specific situation and partly of more general application (e.g. Rom. 12; I Thess. 5.12–22).

Nevertheless, there is a close connection between the topics here and the situation of the church. Topics 1. and 4. are directly related to the disunity in the church and the fear and worry caused by pressure from outside. Topic 2. keeps recurring in the letter and clearly must have been of some local significance. Topic 3. may be connected with the quarrelsomeness in the church which was giving it a bad name in the world generally. Topic 5. is, finally, a general summing up, taking the minds of the readers away from sordid motives to more noble thoughts. It is perhaps the most closely related to the discussion in ch. 3. Note the parallelism between vv. 6f. and 8f.; in each case adopting a certain way of life leads to an experience of the peace of God.

Unity between quarrelling Christians
4.2–3

4.2   In a way that is unparalleled in Paul two specific members of the church are singled out for mention by name for what is in effect a public rebuke in a letter that would have been read aloud to the assembled congregation. The introduction to it in v. 1 softens the harshness that might otherwise be present; it is within the context of Paul's deep love for the church that he is able to speak so directly to its members – a reminder perhaps that plain speaking and discipline should always take place in a context of genuine (and manifest) love for the church.

It is also remarkable that the two people addressed are both women, although we recollect that the first member of the church according to Acts 16 was also a woman. They may have been simply ordinary members of the church, but it is most unlikely that Paul would have spoken directly to them and made a point of their quarrel if it had not been a matter of major concern. It is, therefore, more likely that these two women occupied a place of some importance in the church. What was it?

(a) They had been Paul's *fellow-workers* in the gospel along with his other fellow-workers. This means that they had shared in the work of evangelism, and Paul does not distinguish them as women in any way from other helpers.

(b) They may have been householders in whose homes Christian groups met, and, if so, their rivalry may well have spread to the adherents of their groups. People readily form sides behind their leaders.

(c) It is quite possible that they were included in the 'bishops and deacons' mentioned at the outset of the letter, and that Paul singled out the church leaders for mention there because he had something specific to say to them later.

All this shows that they were in all probability leading members in the church, and therefore their quarrel was all the more serious.

They are therefore counselled to *agree together in the Lord*. Both parts of the phrase are significant. The first repeats what was said in 2.2, and refers to having the same goals, to being like-minded in the sense of having the same broad motives and aims so that they are in harmony with one another. (The word 'harmony' may provide a helpful analogy here. The various voices in a choir do not sing exactly the same notes as one another but they sing notes that fit in euphoniously with one another and that combine to produce a unified effect. Manifestly this analogy was not in Paul's mind, but it may be a helpful parallel in explaining the force of his statement.)

But this harmony must be, second, *in the Lord*. Clearly this refers to some kind of harmony which is through and through Christian. A gang of crooks could be in agreement with one another in their crooked aims and practices. But harmony in the church must be determined by the fact that Jesus is their Lord and they must do what pleases him. So 'in the Lord' characterizes an attitude which is determined by the fact that Christ is the Lord (2.29).

4.3　The instruction to the two women is strengthened by an appeal to a third person to *help* them, i.e. to give them support and so to enable them to reconcile their differences. This may suggest that the two women were on edge as a result of excessive pressure (obviously Paul and the readers knew the situation more fully than we can!) and that the help of a common friend to be a kind of mediator and supporter to both of them would help to resolve the situation.

But who was this helper? We are told that he was a *loyal*, or, rather, true or genuine person, which means that he was a person like Timothy who faithfully followed the ways of his 'father' in the faith (2.20). The word *comrade* suggests that he was one of Paul's helpers resident in Philippi. Commentators attempting to identify him have suggested virtually every Christian known to us by name with connections with Philippi – Luke, Silas, Timothy, Epaphroditus, even Paul's wife (!). One recent suggestion is that this was Paul's way of referring to any individual in the church who hears the letter being read. Alternatively, it is possible that the Greek word is a proper name, *Syzygos*; this is an attractive suggestion but for the difficulties (a) that the name has not yet turned up elsewhere in Greek literature, and (b) that no early church writers (with their knowledge of Greek as a native language) recognized it as a proper name.

The command to help the two women is reinforced by the comment that they are particularly worthy people despite their present differences. They had shared Paul's *struggles* in the gospel. The word used echoes 1.27 with its description of the Philippians as sharing together in the struggle to advance the gospel faith; that may suggest that the two women had been loyal colleagues of Paul in the early days of the mission in Philippi when it had not been easy, but that now, perhaps as a result of their quarrels, they were no longer taking their place with the other members of the church in the struggle. The comment shows incidentally that the local people shared with Paul in the work of evangelism in their own area: they did not stand by and let Paul do all the work.

At that point the two women were also involved with another Christian called *Clement* (a common Latin name – perhaps a Roman citizen?). The mention of the name suggests that he was an outstanding member of the small group that pioneered the gospel in Philippi, and who were closely joined together in Christian fellowship by their common task. Probably Paul is implicitly appealing to the quarrelling women to think back to their harmonious work together in the early days of the church and to strive to recover that spirit once more.

There were others in the group, but Paul does not name them. It is sufficient to comment that all of them have a place in God's book, as people who are members of his church. The *book of life* is a record of those who have eternal life rather than a list of outstanding Christian workers (Luke 10:20; Rev. 3:5). The comment does not imply that these people had already died (cf. Luke 10.20).

WOMEN IN THE CHURCH

The Philippian church is noteworthy for the place of women in it. The description in Acts 16 of its beginnings shows that it started with a group of women; the implication seems to be that there was no synagogue at that time. Euodia and Syntyche were prominent members, as we have seen, and nothing suggests that they occupied roles in any way inferior to those of men in other churches. It may be significant that, where there was apparently no synagogue, and where the more liberal attitudes of the Macedonians may have prevailed, the church developed some female leadership. It may well be that the factor which prevented more widespread development was Jewish influence within other first-century churches. The undoubted fact of such ministry by women, whom Paul highly honoured, shows that the statements elsewhere limiting their activity in the church cannot be taken as universally applicable but probably reflect some local problems.

Joy in the Lord
4.4

4.4   A fresh command is that the readers should rejoice. At least, that is the normal translation of the Greek verb, but here, as in 3.1 the REB interprets it as a wish from Paul. In both places this is a dubious translation. It suggests that Paul is giving a greeting rather than a command. But since the context is one of instructions and commands, this is not very likely.

So what is Paul saying? He is telling them that at all times they should be glad and joyful (cf. I Thess. 5.16), and that the basis of their joy is to be *the Lord* – the joy is that which comes both from recollecting what he has done for them and from their relationship to him. The instruction is important, so Paul emphasizes it by deliberate repetition. Are we to conclude that the Philippian Christians were somewhat downcast because of such various factors as their experience of hostile pressure, their separation from Paul and their concern for him, and their internal divisions? Paul is not simply saying 'Cheer up', but rather, 'Think of the Lord and what he means to you, and that will make you cheerful.' Christian joy is based on what God does for us, not on make-believe.

Sweet reasonableness
4.5

4.5   The next command is probably also concerned with the kind of spirit of divisiveness that was present in the church. It was to be replaced by a spirit of *consideration of others*. This word suggests 'magnanimity', the ability to remain reasonable and unperturbed when confronted by difficult people and to treat them calmly and fairly. Interestingly Paul refers to it as a quality of Jesus himself in II Cor. 10.1 with the implication that his followers are to emulate it. Here it is the opposite of a quarrelsome nature; instead of being irritated by other people, the Christians are to treat difficult people with sweet reasonableness. To say *be known to everyone* is not to suggest that the Christians should parade their magnanimity (to win praise for it) but simply that it should be shown to everybody.

But it is also possible that the attitude is to be shown to difficult people outside the church, even to hostile people and those who attack the church. That is more probably the force of *everyone*. This makes the next clause more meaningful. *The Lord is near* could then mean that, even though the path of meekness is difficult and may not appease hostile people, yet the Lord is near to uphold and vindicate his people.

> The phrase is roughly equivalent to the Aramaic *maranatha* found in I Cor. 16.22 (which may be either a statement or a prayer for the coming of the Lord). Here it is a statement of Christian belief, and it can be interpreted in two ways. On the one hand, it may express belief that the Lord (i.e. Jesus) will soon return as the Son of man and as the Lord. For this belief see Rom. 13.12; James 5.8; Rev. 22.20. Christians are called to be patient, but are assured that it will not be long before the Lord comes to their aid. On the other hand, the phrase could express belief that the unseen presence of the Lord is here and now with his people (Ps. 145.18). It may be that both concepts were in Paul's mind. He may not have distinguished too sharply between the nearness of the Lord in time and in 'space'.

Prayer drives away anxiety and care
4.6–7

4.6 That the situation of hostile pressure is in mind seems to be confirmed by the next instruction which is that the readers are not to be *anxious* (cf. Matt. 6.25ff.). There is a type of anxious concern which is proper for Christians (displayed by Epaphroditus, 2.20), but there is also a kind of concern which is characterized by worried anxiety and lack of faith in the Lord that he will care for his people. It is this second kind which is criticized here. Christians should not worry about the future and fear that things will work out badly. The fact that the Lord is coming is the ultimate basis for their confidence. But here and now rather than worry they should pray to God. Paul piles up the words for prayer here – no less than four of them to express the character of prayer as combining requests and thanks.

(a) Prayer should be said *in everything*, i.e. in every situation. It needs to be said that every situation is an appropriate situation for prayer. People so easily make exceptions because they think prayer is unnecessary (when things are apparently going well) or ineffective (when things seem too difficult) or impossible (because they do not feel in the mood to pray).

(b) It should include *thanksgiving*. The people who pray remember what God has already done and is doing for them and show their gratitude. At the same time, the recollection of answered prayers gives them confidence to make further requests. If God is faithful and consistent, he will continue to show his concern for them as he has in time past.

(c) It includes specific *requests*. Prayer is not merely a general expression of confidence in God. It can be quite detailed as particular needs are brought before God.

4.7   When people pray in this kind of way, one of the fruits of it will be *the peace of God* in their lives. This is something more than human peace, and indeed there is a sense in which it lies beyond our understanding (like God's power, Eph 3.20). Paul evidently means more than simply a feeling of well-being, and thinks rather of the wholeness and salvation which comes from God and, so to speak, takes possession of people (cf. Col. 3.15). It acts like a garrison in a fortress, to *guard* and provide protection from outside dangers. In this case it is the minds and thoughts of the believers which are defended from having the wrong kinds of thoughts – anxiety and faithlessness are put to flight.

Can we push the metaphor to say that God's peace is in effect like a peace-keeping force, a body of soldiers who take possession of an area and keep it safe from outside attacks, thereby producing safety and security inside? Note the last phrase, *in Christ Jesus*; it surely means that God's peace like all his other blessings comes to us through Jesus Christ (through whom we have our relationship with him), and it spells out that this particular blessing of peace is for Christian believers.

That may be important to stress. Much that passes for Christianity consists of a rather general faith in God without any specific relationship to the Christian revelation. People have a conviction that God will look after them and care for them through his general providential care. It is an interesting question how far such a general sort of faith is justified. For in the NT the channel of God's blessing is always Jesus, and the idea that one can enjoy God's peace apart from a relationship of trust in Jesus seems to be excluded. How far, then, is the broad 'trust in God' which many people have justified? Would it be true to say that people who have such a trust should be encouraged to recognize that Christ is the channel of God's blessings, and that people who have a true faith in God will show that it is such by gladly accepting Christ when he is presented to them?

The Christian's thoughts
4.8–9

4.8 The last item in this list of commands is introduced by *And now*.

This is translated 'finally' in some versions; if that is correct, it introduces the last item in this series of instructions and not necessarily the end of the letter. In fact, it may be simply a way of moving from one point to another.

It is a remarkable instruction both because of its content and because it is not easy to see what its function is in the letter.

The content is clear enough. We have two separate, but related commands. The first is concerned with the thinking of the readers. They are to contemplate or meditate on the kind of things that Paul lists. The second is concerned with their behaviour, which is to be based on what they have received and seen in the church. There is thus something of a contrast between the two commands, and this strengthens the view that the former command is concerned with the standards of the world in general.

Paul writes on the assumption that there are things which are *excellent and admirable*. The former word refers to that quality which makes anything good for its intended purpose and so to virtue in general. The latter word refers to what is worthy of praise. Both words cover what is regarded as being of quality and value in the world. It follows that if there are such things, which are regarded as being good and better than other things, then people should cherish them rather than things which are evil and imperfect. Paul lists the kind of things which show these qualities and would be universally recognized by right-minded people. They hardly require individual comment. *Noble* refers to things that gain respect, 'highly esteemed because of their honourable nature'. *Pure* conveys the idea of actions that do not make a person defiled and dirty in the sight of God. *Lovable* means 'attractive', things that are admirable. The meanings of the words thus overlap considerably. They combine to convey the idea of things that are honourable and therefore attractive.

Paul is thinking of things and deeds which fall into these categories rather than of people who display these qualities. So he could be thinking of examples of moral goodness in human behaviour or of objects in nature and art that are attractive. These are to be the objects of Christian thinking. The problem in the verse is whether Paul is thinking primarily in moral or aesthetic terms. The emphasis seems to be on the former, but the scope seems greater than morally good actions. Paul is not far off saying 'Fill your minds with what is beautiful rather than with what is ugly.'

4.9   To complete the picture Paul refers to a second set of things which are church-oriented. These are things to be done or practised, and they include things which the readers have seen in Paul; he must, therefore, be thinking primarily of a way of behaviour which he has exemplified. The earlier part of the list contains what they have been taught in various ways. What the readers have *learned* is obviously the content of Christian instruction. The second word *received* refers to material which is handed down as tradition. That is to say, it is material which had come down to Paul or other teachers from other Christians; it was generally recognized as authoritative in the church, and it would be taught with relatively little variation, whereas what they *learned* could include teaching given by Paul (or others) that was not necessarily so universally accepted. REB takes what they had *heard* as another way of referring to this same body of material but stressing that it had come from the lips of Paul, whereas by contrast what they had *seen* would indicate that they had seen for themselves that Paul practised what he preached. It is also possible that what they had heard was not what Paul himself taught but rather what people said about his behaviour when he himself was not present (for example, somebody like Timothy visiting the church).

This second sentence thus confirms that what Paul is thinking of is primarily behaviour. He wants the readers to think about whatever is morally good and attractive and to put into practice both these things and the specific Christian instruction received in the church.

Why is the instruction here in this letter? It seems probable that Paul is anxious about the examples of unlovely conduct in the church, about people being self-centred and quarrelsome, proud and earthy, and therefore he is urging the readers to fill their thoughts with whatever is good in conduct, and to practise it. Thus this section is the antidote to the attitudes criticized earlier in the letter.

Finally, there is the promise that (if they live in this manner) *the God of peace* will be with them. This means that the God who loves and promotes peace will be present in a church where there is unity and peace between the members, and they will be conscious of his blessings. It is in effect saying that where people do not live in peace and harmony, the God who loves peace is excluded by their conduct and they will not receive his blessings.

DIVINE BLESSINGS

The application of all this to the church is straightforward, and no 'translation' is required. The problem for many people is the question of 'divine blessing'. There is no doubt that in the Bible generally there is the belief that, if people trust in God and do his will (as expressed in his commandments), they will experience 'blessing'; conversely, if they do not do so, if, for example, their church life is riddled by quarrelling, then they will not experience God's blessing and may even experience some kind of negative experience.

This teaching exists side by side with other teaching which insists that if evil befalls people, it is not necessarily a sign of God's displeasure, and that suffering may be the experience of God's people simply because they live in a world where evil is rampant.

It is not easy to reduce this teaching to a tidy system, and many modern people question whether God is the kind of person who apportions blessing and disaster on the basis of the individual good or evil actions of people. We may be happy with the thought that God rewards those who serve him faithfully. But what about the other side? Is there ever a situation where we might claim today that a particular disaster hitting a Christian group (the bolt of lightning that set a cathedral on fire or the fatal illness of an individual) was a judgment upon their sin? Clearly, there can be cases where a particular way of life is the direct cause of a a particular result (where, for example, people who smoke heavily should not be surprised if they get lung cancer, or where a builder who skimps his work finds that his house collapses in a storm); but even in these cases Christians might want to claim that God may or may not allow these natural results to follow. But what is at issue here is the problem of both blessings and disasters that are not *directly caused* by a particular form of conduct but might be interpreted as embodying a divine response to it. Is it right to think in these terms? It would surely be intolerable to say that we cannot have special experiences of God's blessing in our lives or that prayers to him (e.g. in the midst of danger) make no difference. Equally, however, we have no right to interpret a particular disaster as a divine judgment upon somebody for their sin, although we can point out in general terms that God can speak to us through such events. Above all, we can, however, draw attention to the good things that happen in people's lives and encourage them to view them as evidences of God's grace to them which invite their faith and gratitude.

Thanks for a gift to Paul
4.10–20

Paul is approaching the end of his letter, and therefore he turns to matters of a more personal nature. He expresses his thanks at some length for the gift which Epaphroditus had brought to him from Philippi and makes some general comments on the matter.

It has been thought strange that Paul reserves his comments on the gift to a point so late in the letter, and this is one of the reasons why it has been argued that 4.10–20 is really part of a separate letter which was sent as soon as the gift was received. But, as we have noted earlier, Paul had already referred to the gift in 1.4f. and indirectly in 2.25–30; he now develops his thanks more fully after dealing with the more pressing problems regarding his own situation and that of the church. Parallels from his other letters show that Paul tended to deal with personal matters of this kind at the end of a letter. There is at least one secular letter which shows the same pattern of holding back thanks for a gift to the end of the letter.

Advocates of reading the letter as a rhetorical composition argue that the purpose of this section is to secure sympathy for Paul and so encourage the readers to heed his injunctions in the main part of the letter. But this interpretation smacks of trying to force the material into a predetermined mould, and it is better to take it at its face value as a piece of personal communication.

The paragraph is concerned to say two main things:
(1) Paul is grateful for the gift which represents feelings of affection that the church had been unable for some reason to express tangibly for some time (although they had helped him in the early days of his work in Macedonia), and he knows that God will regard their gift to him with favour and bless them accordingly.
(2) Paul explains that, if there had been times when he had not had sufficient during the period before their gift came, this does not mean that he was complaining; in fact he had learned how to live cheerfully in whatever circumstances. Some commentators have

118

taken this to mean that Paul was in effect saying that, although he was grateful for the gift, nevertheless he could do without it and he did not really want gifts of this kind for his work. He would accept help of other kinds but not gifts to him personally. This suggestion is far from convincing, and we shall see how it fares against a more detailed examination of the passage.

4.10 Paul's reaction on receiving a gift for his work was to have *joy… in the Lord*. This means that he traced the action of his friends to the influence of the Lord, and that he was grateful to the Lord and rejoiced because of what he had done. Some commentators have suggested that Paul was not thankful to the Philippians and avoided saying thanks to them. This is a misunderstanding. Surely Paul could scarcely express his joy at what they had done any more strongly than he does here. Admittedly, his words may give the impression that their concern for him had been at low ebb and had just recently sprung into life after some time. But Paul himself seems to have felt that he had expressed himself clumsily, and therefore he corrected himself immediately by saying that it was not the thought that was lacking on their part but the opportunity to help him. When he says that their concern had *revived*, what he really means is that it had 'blossomed afresh'. The metaphor does not suggest that it had died, but rather that it was like a plant waiting for the right weather conditions to burst into flower. We do not know why the church had had no opportunity to help Paul. If, for example, he had been taken captive and then transferred to Rome, there could have been a lengthy period when they did not know just where he was, or were waiting to see what would happen to him. Or it may be that they temporarily lacked the necessary financial resources.

4.11 Paul is very anxious to avoid the impression that he was making any kind of criticism of his friends for not helping him. Although he was glad to receive their gift, this was not because of a sense of want and deprivation which he thought that his friends had a duty to relieve. On the contrary he had learned by experience to be *self-sufficient*. Here the translation may suggest that Paul had learned to depend on himself and so to insulate himself from his circumstances. Such an attitude was found among the Stoic philosophers who consciously cultivated it. But the context shows that Paul did not depend upon himself and his own resources, but upon Christ, and the older translation 'content' (NIV) gives a better idea of what he meant. He was able to be happy, whatever happened to him, because he was persuaded that a God who loved him and cared for him was in charge of the situation and he could rejoice in whatever happened to him.

4.12   He could therefore say that he knew by experience what it was *to have nothing* or *plenty* – both experiences had happened to him at different times. But many people can know what it is to have these experiences without knowing how to cope with them. When Paul says that he has been *thoroughly initiated*, he may mean not just that he has had ample experience of these states but also that he had learned the secret of how to cope with being full or hungry, well-off or poor. Both kinds of situation bring their temptations – the one perhaps to live carelessly and the other to despair and be dejected. Paul felt that he could overcome in either situation.

4.13   Then he explains how this is possible: He had the strength to cope with either kind of situation in the person who gave him power. *Anything* must be understood in its context. It basically refers to both extremes of situation, and it can be enlarged to mean that Paul can cope with all sorts of difficulty; it does not mean that he could do literally everything. But it does mean that he could face up to temptations, to distress, to the threat of death, and so on, without being overcome by them. And the source of his strength was Christ, here described as the person who gives him the power that he needs. Human analogies suggest perhaps the picture of a child who can face problems and difficulties with greater success with the help and encouragement of a father who shows what to do, encourages, and is present to spur on and applaud, and perhaps also to actively help. (Think of the small child saying, 'I can't jump off the wall unless you're there to catch me, Dad.') In the same kind of way Paul claimed a relationship with Christ that gave him the strength and resources that he needed.

4.14   Despite this sense of being able to face up to different circumstances, Paul did not find the gift any the less welcome – especially when he believed that such gifts were ultimately due to the grace of God. He was glad at what the Philippian Christians had done for him. By their action they had shared *the burden of his troubles*. This can mean that they themselves actually shared in Paul's affliction with him by undergoing the sacrifice of giving him some of their

money and thus having less than they needed for their own requirements; or it may simply mean that they felt sympathy for Paul in his
affliction and showed it by their gift.

4.15 In fact, they had been doing this for some time. It may seem
strange that Paul says *You Philippians are aware* regarding something
that they themselves had done. But the point is not that they had
been helping Paul but that they had been the only church to do so.
Their assistance to him went right back to *the early days* of his
mission. Paul had, of course, been busy as a missionary long before
the Philippians had ever heard of him, and therefore this phrase
must be used from their point of view, to refer to the time when Paul
was first active in their part of the world. After Paul left Philippi and
Thessalonica, he had gone south into Greece proper, to Athens and
Corinth, and there he had initially to found churches from nothing.
There was therefore no support for him from local Christians, but
the Philippian church had sent help to him (II Cor. 11.9 refers to this
or to similar help). They had behaved like partners in a business
arrangement. This is the picture present in the language, but it also
reflects the thought of Christian fellowship. The *giving and receiving*
can refer to the money given by the church and to the spiritual
benefits from Paul's teaching which they received (cf. Gal 6.6).
Alternatively, it may simply mean that they gave the money and
Paul received it.

4.16 In fact, even before Paul left Macedonia and had only moved
on as far as Thessalonica they had sent him gifts more than once.
Here Paul does indicate that he had needs that would not otherwise
have been met. So we must take v. 12 quite seriously. He did know
what it was to lack the necessities of life – food, perhaps shelter and
clothing, and other comforts. But sometimes he was able to supply
his needs, either by his own work with his hands (Acts 20.34) or
thanks to gifts from the church.

4.17 Once again Paul makes it clear that he is not looking for gifts –
he can do without them, and his policy had been to work with his
hands so as not to be a burden to anybody (I Cor. 9; I Thess. 2). But
the gift has another effect. It produces a return of a different kind.
Jesus taught his disciples that by giving away their earthly goods
they would gain for themselves treasure in heaven. So Paul says that
the demonstration of this generous act by the Philippian Christians

121

would lead to credit for them in the sight of God that would grow and increase. He uses the picture of a capital sum of money earning interest to make the point. The commercial metaphor used in v. 15 is found again here. Paul's real desire is that the gifts of his friends should achieve something for themselves personally rather than for himself.

4.18 Nevertheless, Paul cannot refrain from expressing appreciation for what they have given him. He has been *paid in full*. Again the language of commerce is used: he is like a person who is signing a receipt acknowledging that full payment has been received. As a consequence he is now in the position which he described in v. 12b; he has all that he needs – and even more. And perhaps there is the idea that when God does give more than he needs he can enjoy it and rejoice in it.

At the same time he repeats the thought that the gift is really made to God. It is likened to a *sacrifice* that God is pleased to receive. We recall that not all sacrifices in the ancient world were means of dealing with sin; many were offered as thank offerings or in payment of vows to God. They expressed the obligation of the worshippers to God and their freewill offerings. This is what Paul has in mind here. The Philippians' gift to him was the kind of thing that God was pleased to receive.

4.19 It followed that God would show his favour to them. He would supply all their needs. The thought is presumably not confined to spiritual needs; the Philippian Christians could also have material needs like Paul, and God could use other Christians to help them, as they had helped Paul. Perhaps there is the thought that if they had impoverished themselves by helping Paul, and if he himself could not help them, then God would use other people to provide for their needs. Thus willingness to give sacrificially to help others would not put the givers to disadvantage. God will see to it that they do not go uncared for or unrewarded. And God's giving is on a lavish scale. He supplies *out of the magnificence of his riches* – on a scale worthy of his wealth, says one writer.

4.20 The thought of all this makes Paul break out in praise to God for his goodness. He uses a traditional form of words in describing God as *our Father*, and he follows a traditional practice in bursting into a doxology to God in this way. The Jewish Rabbis often used the formula 'The Holy One – blessed be he – ...' which could become stereotyped and therefore almost meaningless. Here Paul deliberately means what he says.

CHRISTIAN GIVING

Reading this passage as preachers, we note that it demands attention in thinking about Christian giving, and specifically about giving for the mission of the church.

The balance between the divine and the human in church finance is not an easy one. The church says: 'We are looking to the Lord to supply our needs for the extension to the church hall', but it also says at the same time: 'We ask you to be generous in your giving to this worthy cause. Ask the Lord how much he wants you to give to this project.' Is there a tension between these statements?

(a) We want to see people being generous because this is a sign of their growth in grace. The Philippian church stands out as a noble example in this respect.

(b) The Philippians showed sympathy and understanding of Paul's situation. Christian workers cannot live on nothing. Often people don't give aid because they don't know that a need exists. By one means or another the Philippians knew that Paul was in need, and so they acted.

(c) Some people find the whole idea of Christian fund-raising distasteful. Is it right to use commercial methods of fund-raising in the church? The answer to this question may lie in recognizing that a Christian employed in secular fund-raising would endeavour to do so in a Christian manner. There will be some practices which are acceptable and others which are not. Surely the same general principles would then be applied in fund-raising for the church and for Christian causes.

(d) Finally, we must learn to be content with what the Lord gives – or does not give – us.

Closing greetings
4.21–23

The personal conclusion to the letter, probably written by Paul in his own hand, is quite brief. Essentially it consists of a set of greetings from Paul and two groups of people who are with him, which culminate in the expression of a prayer to God for the recipients.

4.21 Paul's own greeting is in the form of a command to the readers to *give my greetings… to each one of God's people*. The thought may be that the church leaders are to make sure that everybody, including those not present when the letter is read, hears that Paul sends his love to them. It is important that nobody is to be excluded – Paul explicitly says not 'all God's people' but 'each one of God's people' – and this may be significant in a divided church: Paul is not taking sides, but includes everybody in his embrace. *In the fellowship of Christ Jesus* (cf. Rom. 16.22) indicates that it is a Christian greeting which is being conveyed, and therefore it is different in some way from a non-Christian or secular one. It is a recognition that they all stand within the circle of God's people. (It is possible that the phrase describes 'each one of God's people' rather than indicating the way in which the greetings are to be conveyed.)

Second, the *colleagues* (lit. 'brothers') who are with Paul also send greetings. These are the people engaged in missionary work alongside him who are distinguished from 'all God's people here'. This may seem to raise a problem in that 2.20f. may have suggested that Paul had no like-minded colleagues. However, this note will include Timothy (2.19) and the people who were proclaiming Christ from good motives (1.15b, 16).

4.22 Third, *all God's people here* send greetings. This includes especially *those in the emperor's service*. This phrase refers to members of what we would call the 'civil service' or the government administration in Rome, or (if the letter was written elsewhere) it could refer to people who worked for the governor of a province in his residence. But why are they mentioned especially? We can only speculate. Possibly some of them travelled in pursuit of their business and had visited Philippi and become acquainted with the members of the church. Or it may simply be that a group of Christians in this service had got together and developed an interest in this particular area of the world: was there a 'Philippi prayer-meeting' held in some government office in Rome?

4.23   Then the letter concludes with a benediction which is also found word for word in Philemon 25, and in a fuller form in Gal. 6.18. Paul in fact ends all his letters with a prayer like this for divine grace to be with the recipients. But why *with your spirit*? Paul does make some kind of distinction between the physical and the spiritual sides of human nature, and therefore it is natural enough for him to express his prayer in this kind of way. He could have said simply 'be with you', as he does in other letters, but this expression brings out the fact that he sees grace operating in our spiritual nature. Thus the letter begins and ends with grace. It is the grace of *our Lord Jesus Christ*. He is so much the channel of all the good gifts that come to us that it was not necessary for Paul specifically to mention God the Father here.

FINALLY, MY FRIENDS

Here we are, then, at the end of the letter. How would you sum up the main points that we have found in it that are important for a modern congregation? Can you preach a relevant series of sermons from Philippians – or even one sermon that sums up the message of a book that, after all, was probably read in one go by the original readers?

   Maybe the starting-point is a Bible study group in which people engage in a dialogue with the text and discover how it speaks to them. Your church may not have the problems of disunity that Paul found at Philippi. It will almost certainly not be threatened by Judaizers, although it may well contain people who feel that they have 'arrived' spiritually. It may not know what it is to be persecuted, although at least some of the congregation may be too timid to express their faith in the outside world. And perhaps there are people who do not find the letter at all on their wavelength with so much of its theology based on the depiction of a being who emptied himself and became a man.

Can we share the basis of Paul's theology and the consequent practical teaching? The centre of the letter is undoubtedly the passage (2.6–11) which speaks of the original state of Christ before the incarnation, the choice attributed to him, his becoming a human being, and his exaltation to be with God the Father again. Some people would describe this language as 'mythological' and argue that it cannot be used as a basis for Christian thinking today.

Although the word 'mythological' is sometimes used to refer to material taken over from ancient myths, it is generally agreed that this passage is not based on such material. Rather, the word is used in this context to refer to the use of human language and ideas to express realities outside the human world, and, in particular, to speak of divine beings in human terms. For some people such a use of language is frankly imaginative and even misleading, in that it appears to suggest that God can be described – and described adequately – in human terms, and therefore, they argue, it should be dropped.

For some interpreters the problem does not arise in so sharp a form, because in their view the hymn is not about the career of Christ before his human birth but rather about the human choice that he made not to follow the path chosen by Adam. For those, however, who take the view defended in this commentary, namely that the pre-existence of Christ is being depicted, the problem cannot be evaded, and in any case all interpreters have to cope with the language of exaltation and what that implies. Is the passage simply an imaginative way of expressing the deep humiliation and supreme position of Christ, using the language of praise rather than doctrine?

One possibility is that what we have here is a way of putting the understanding of Jesus as the 'son of God' which we find elsewhere in the NT, both in Paul (e.g. Rom. 8.32; Gal. 4.4) and especially in John (e.g. 3.16), and which arose from knowledge of Jesus' self-consciousness as the Son of the Father (Matt. 11.25–27). Language already existed in the Old Testament and Judaism (e.g. Prov. 8.22–31) to describe the role of wisdom alongside God before the creation of the world and wisdom's departure into the world of mankind. This was picked up and used as a vehicle for describing the role of the Son, but now it was used in a much more personal way instead of being simply personification. Such guage can be used, despite all the attendant risks, to express realities too deep for human words; provided that it is recognized that it is not necessarily to be taken as literal and exhaustive in its reference, it is an appropriate vehicle to use in Christian theology and teaching. The language of persons and personal relationships is the most adequate that we possess to speak about God. If it be true that human beings are made in the image of God, we may rightly claim that the kind of language which we use about ourselves can also – with all due recognition of its inadequacy – be used analogically of the divine Trinity.

Along such lines we may defend Paul's understanding of Jesus as still being meaningful in the modern world. Its importance is then that Paul discusses human problems by constant reference to Jesus – to his role as a Saviour who has conquered death and will enable us to triumph over it; to his position as an Example who has demonstrated how we are to live in humility and self-giving for the sake of others; and to his status as the Lord to whom we must render obedience. Above all else, perhaps, Philippians stresses what we have called the cruciform life, a pattern of living that arises out of our relationship to a crucified and resurrected Lord. He calls those who commit their lives to him to share both in his self-denial and readiness to suffer for the sake of other people and also at the same time in the power of the new life that is a foretaste of God's new world, an 'antepast of heaven' (as Charles Wesley put it). This gives a new perspective to the whole of human living and dying.

The preacher will also note the stress on such integrally related points as:

loving unity within the church, beginning with the local congregation;

generous giving to the needs of others (not least those who go out in the Lord's service, giving up a regular income and trusting that the Lord will provide for their needs through his people);

sharing the good news of Jesus Christ with a world in which (as in Paul's time) there are many religions but where it is still at the name of Jesus Christ that everybody must fall down and worship. To proclaim him as Lord and Saviour is still the preacher's highest privilege and duty.